D1825650

THE

𝕷𝖎𝖙𝖙𝖑𝖊 𝕽𝖊𝖉 𝕭𝖔𝖔𝖐

OF THE

HISTORY

OF THE

HOLY CATHOLIC CHURCH

IN IRELAND.

BY

ROBERT KING, A.B.

Curate of the Six-towns, Ballynascreen,

AUTHOR OF "A PRIMER OF THE CHURCH HISTORY OF IRELAND," ETC.

DUBLIN
JAMES McGLASHAN, 21 D'OLIER-STREET.
WM. S. ORR AND CO., 147 STRAND, LONDON.
MDCCCXLVIII.

In the interest of creating a more extensive selection of rare historical book reprints, we have chosen to reproduce this title even though it may possibly have occasional imperfections such as missing and blurred pages, missing text, poor pictures, markings, dark backgrounds and other reproduction issues beyond our control. Because this work is culturally important, we have made it available as a part of our commitment to protecting, preserving and promoting the world's literature. Thank you for your understanding.

TO THE

MASTERS AND SENIOR SCHOLARS

OF THE

NATIONAL AND OTHER SCHOOLS

IN IRELAND AND GREAT BRITAIN,

𝕮𝖍𝖎𝖘 𝖑𝖎𝖙𝖙𝖑𝖊 𝖂𝖔𝖗𝖐

IS RESPECTFULLY DEDICATED, IN THE HOPE

THAT THEY MAY FIND IT

A USEFUL MANUAL OF INFORMATION,

ON A VERY IMPORTANT

BUT HITHERTO MUCH NEGLECTED

BRANCH OF STUDY.

A

𝔓𝔯𝔢𝔣𝔞𝔠𝔢.

———•———

THAT the subject of the present work is one
in regard to which very gross ignorance has
hitherto been generally prevalent, is a fact which
no person of a reasonable disposition can for a
moment hesitate to admit. That very great errors
and serious mischiefs have arisen from such ignorance, must also be pretty evident to any person of
moderate learning and candour. And that no sufficient means has yet been provided for supplying,
generally, the information needed in order to re-
move this ignorance, and the errors rooted in it,
is almost equally apparent.

These circumstances will sufficiently account for
the appearance of the present work—designed, not
as an attempt perfectly to supply the existing
want, but as a contribution to the purpose, which,
in its humble sphere of usefulness, will share, perhaps, with other productions of superior minds,
the honour of helping to dispel some portion of the
cloudy mist which has heretofore veiled from us,
in obscurity, the venerable face of Irish ecclesiastical
antiquity.

It is among the people at large that such ignorance and errors as are above specified have most
prevailed. For the people generally, therefore,
this little book is intended; with which object in
view, it has been compiled in a plain and simple
style, adapted to the apprehension of the most ignorant and unlearned. For the benefit of such, has
also been introduced the general matter contained
in the first seven chapters of the work; the sacred
volume· from which it has been collected being
too often a sealed record to many of those to whom
the present compilation may be useful.

The facts of history plainly stated, as in this
little book, are certainly intelligible enough to the
meanest capacity. The *most ignorant*, however,
cannot be the *best* judges of such matters; too
often it happens that the ignorant love and venerate
ignorance, regarding it with the feeling of fosterage-
affection proper towards the nursing mother of the
errors which they cherish and adore. To expect
that such persons should best appreciate the importance and value of historical truth, were unreason-
able indeed. Even those of them who are of more
candid minds, may see *something* of its importance,
understand something of its connexion with their
own position and conduct; but only to be per-
plexed at what they read, and led to look with

anxious eye to those better informed than themselves, to inquire, "are these things so?"

To the better informed and more intelligent classes, therefore, we would more particularly address ourselves herein—to those first to whom the work is dedicated; then to all who are considered to occupy among their countrymen stations of any little superior importance—poor-law guardians, medical practitioners, chapel committee-men, repeal-wardens — all, in fact, who are leaders in their little spheres; all who, having a better education and more enlightened minds, take an interest in the matter, and care for the difference between truth and error.

To such persons, a word in conclusion. Shrouded as this subject has been in ignorance—confused with error—it is natural to anticipate that some of the views here set forth will appear new and strange to you, as they have appeared to others before you—even to men in other points most learned—who, however, on deeper and more careful examination, have been led to embrace and adopt, as most undeniably certain, those positions which at first struck them as startling and improbable. Give them, however, but a fair inquiry, as thinking, intelligent men—as those to whose opinions others look for guidance—as men worthy to be guides—men not afraid of the facts of history. Compare the statements here made, with those of the best reputed authorities within your reach ; see how far they agree—observe where they differ, what the probable occasion of the discrepancy, and what its importance. And may the Fountain of all illumination and wisdom bless the result, in increasing in you the knowledge and love of that which is in accordance with truth.

*** It is respectfully suggested that such of the Gentry and Clergy throughout the country as approve of this little work, and feel an interest in the subject, may greatly promote its utility, by presenting copies to the various National School Teachers, Poor Law Guardians, &c. &c., in their parishes or on their estates.

Contents.

THE

𝕷𝖎𝖙𝖙𝖑𝖊 𝕽𝖊𝖉 𝕭𝖔𝖔𝖐

OF THE

HISTORY OF THE HOLY CATHOLIC CHURCH IN IRELAND.

—❈❈❈—

Chap. I.—Of the World, from the Creation to the Deluge.

B.C. 4004–2349.

IN the beginning God created the heavens and the earth, and all things that are in them, in six days. And God created man also, and placed him upon the earth, 4004 years before that our Saviour Jesus Christ was born into the world. The first man was called Adam, and the name of his wife was Eve; and from those two were descended all that afterwards lived on the whole earth. Adam and Eve were created holy and happy, and placed at first in the beautiful garden of Eden, to live there. But when they were led, by the temptation of Satan, to eat of the forbidden fruit, for this act of disobedience against God, his displeasure fell upon them; they were expelled

B

from the paradise of Eden; death entered into the
world; and that one sin was the cause and beginning
of all the trouble and sorrow which has fallen to the
lot of man since their day.

In the course of time, the descendants of Adam and
Eve became very numerous, and began to spread all
over the face of the whole earth: but they also became very wicked, and provoked God's anger more
and more. At length, in the time of Noah, 2439
years before the birth of Christ, the Almighty sent a
flood of waters on the earth, which swept away mankind and all other things from off the face of the
world, and drowned them all. God gave them notice
that such destruction was coming on them, if they
would not repent, and turn from their wicked ways.
But although they got this notice 120 years before the
flood came, none of them repented, nor paid attention
to the word of God, excepting only Noah. All the
rest went on, eating and drinking, buying and selling,
planting and building, marrying and giving their children in marriage as usual, until the day when the flood
came, and destroyed them all. But Noah, having
faith in God, found favour in his sight, and took the
warning that was given him, and prepared the ark,
according to the directions received from on high.
And when the deluge came, he and his family went
into the ark, and were saved from the waters. They
were eight persons in all, *i. e.*, Noah himself, and his
three sons, who were called Shem, Ham, and Japhet,
and their four wives. And at the beginning of the

deluge it rained for forty days and forty nights. And for 150 days the waters prevailed over the face of the earth, before they began to abate and dry away.

Chap. II.—The Call of Abraham.

B.C. 1921.

WHEN the earth was dry once more, Noah and his family came forth from the ark again, after they had lived in it about one year. And when they came out, God blessed them, and gave them a promise that he would never again send a flood of waters on the earth any more. And he appointed the rainbow in heaven to be a sign of that promise, so long as the world should last. After this the descendants of Noah, in the course of time, multiplied greatly on the earth, and began to cover the face of the world with people once more. But men forgot God again, and made little of his mighty power, and continued still to provoke his anger by their sins. Even Ham, the son of Noah, who was himself saved in the ark, showed an example of wickedness after the flood was gone, and brought a curse on himself for his impiety. So that we do not so much wonder to find that in about 400 years after the flood most of the inhabitants of the world had gone far astray from God, and were following idolatry and false religion.

But there was one man of those who lived about this time, who loved God, and firmly believed in his word ; and he was called Abraham. And his faith

in God was so strong, and his life so good, that the
Almighty caused the history of it to be written down
in the Bible, for an example to all that should come
after. And Abraham obtained the name of the Father
of the faithful, and the friend of God. Now when
Abraham was living in his own country, among his
own idolatrous friends, it pleased God to call him
from that place into a strange land named Canaan,
1921 years before the birth of Christ. And Abraham
immediately did as God commanded him, and came
and lived in Canaan. And afterwards God promised
that he would give him the whole country of Canaan
for his own family, and it accordingly came to them,
as we shall see presently, in the course of time. But
there were many remarkable things to happen to the
family before this came to pass.

To Abraham, when he was ninety years old, God,
according to his promise, gave a son called Isaac,
who became inheritor of the blessings which had
been promised to his father. And the son of Isaac,
who succeeded to the inheritance of the same blessings, was named Jacob.

Chap. III.—Of Joseph and his Brethren.

B.C. 1720.

NOW it pleased God to give Jacob twelve sons, who are called also the twelve patriarchs, that is, the heads of twelve great families, because twelve great families or tribes were afterwards descended from them. And their names are these: Reuben, Simeon, Levi, Judah, Zebulon, Issachar, Dan, Gad, Asher, Napthali, Joseph, and Benjamin. And because Jacob loved his young son Joseph beyond the rest, when he was old, the elder brothers were envious, and had some thought of killing Joseph. However, they sold him for a slave to some people going by their place, who were travelling down to Egypt. And so Joseph was brought with them to Egypt: and there he was put in prison for a false accusation. But God was with him, and saved him out of all his trouble, and brought him into great favour with Pharaoh, king of Egypt, and with all his people. For there was a great famine coming on the world, and God Almighty gave notice of it beforehand to Pharaoh, by means of Joseph, so that they were able to gather great stores of corn and food of all kinds in Egypt. And when the famine came, it lasted for seven years. But while they were starving in other places, the people of Egypt had enough, so that men came from other parts, far and near, to buy

from them in Egypt. And Joseph's brethren came
down from Canaan to Egypt for food; and he was
good and kind to them, and forgave them all their
ill-treatment of himself, and got places in Egypt for
them to live in, where they might have plenty; and
his father Jacob too came down, and settled at that
time in the same country: and the descendants of
Jacob grew to a very large number in that place.
But after a good while, when Jacob was nearly two
hundred years dead, the Egyptians began to hate
and persecute his descendants very bitterly, and
their king brought in a law that every boy that was
born to them should be killed, that they might
multiply no more. And the Egyptians put them to
hard labour, making slaves of them, and keeping
them at brick-making, and building, and other such
employments, with very cruel treatment.

Chap. IV.—*How Moses and Aaron led the People of Israel out of Egypt.*

B.C. 1491.

GOD gave to Jacob the name of Israel, from
which his descendants were called Israelites,
or the children of Israel. They are also sometimes
called Hebrews, from Abraham their forefather, who
had the name of the Hebrew; and it is in their
language (that is, the Hebrew) that the Bible, the
most ancient book in the world, is written. Now,

when these Israelites were in very great hardship in
Egypt, as we have said already, God Almighty did
not forget the promise he had made to their forefather
Abraham, concerning the good things he was to do
for them in after time in the land of Canaan. And
therefore he raised up Moses to be their deliverer, to
bring them away out of the land of Egypt, which was
to them a house of bondage.

When Moses was born, his parents hid him three
months, because they saw him to be so fine a child:
and at last when they were obliged to put him out,
Pharoah's daughter found him, and brought him
home to the king's house, and had him brought up
very carefully. But when he grew to be a man, he did
not care about living with Pharoah, because he loved
his own people, and it grieved him sadly to see them
suffering such hardships. But God appeared to him,
and told him that he was to bring the people out of
Egypt, and gave him power to work many terrible
miracles among the Egyptians, and send very awful
plagues upon them, for their disobedience to God,
and persecution of his people. At last it came to
pass that Pharaoh and the Egyptians resolved to let
the people go, because they were sore afraid of them,
and of the miracles they had seen. And so Moses
and his brother Aaron led the people out of Egypt
by night, about 600,000 that were men, besides children. This was about 400 years after the time of
God's promise to Abraham, and 1,491 years before
the birth of Christ our Saviour. After the people

had left Egypt, God wrought another great miracle
for them at the Red Sea; for he brought them
through its waters on a dry path. But when Pharoah
and the Egyptians attempted to pursue them, they
were all drowned, and perished in the same waters.

Chap. V.—The Settlement of Israel in the land of Canaan.

B. C. 1451.

AFTER passing through the Red Sea, the Israelites came into the wilderness of Mount Sinai.
And there on that mountain God gave them, by the
hand of Moses, the Ten Commandments, and many
other useful and holy laws. But they were continually provoking him to anger, by discontent, and murmuring, and idolatry, and other abominable sins.
For they presumed to worship the Lord God by
means of an image, which he had forbidden in the
Ten Commandments. And so for their murmuring
and unbelief, God swore in his wrath that they should
not enter into the land of promise. And he kept
them in the wilderness forty years, until all that
generation had passed away. And after that, Joshua,
who succeeded to Moses as their leader, brought them
into the land of Canaan. And God gave them power
to overcome the seven wicked nations that inhabited
that land, and to get possession of that country for
themselves. And they and their children lived there
afterwards, from generation to generation.

And in Canaan the Israelites enjoyed many and great privileges and blessings. They had a fine rich and fruitful country, stored with all good things, and flowing with milk and honey. And what was better than all beside, they had the true knowledge of God among them, and the reading and hearing of his Word, when all the other nations of the earth were living in darkness and ignorance, and following their own ways, or rather walking in the broad way that leadeth to destruction. But God Almighty sent to them from time to time many prophets and teachers, to call them to repentance, and instruct them in the right ways of the Lord. But the people were mostly disobedient and rebellious, and gave little heed to their good instructions. On their first coming into Canaan, and for nearly 300 years after, they were governed by judges and law-givers, until the time of Samuel the prophet: but from that out they had kings over them, the first of whom was called Saul.

Chap. VI.—*Of the Temple of Solomon, &c.*

B. C. 1012–536.

THE second King of Israel, whose name was called David, was a very great and famous prophet, and wrote many psalms by the inspiration of the Holy Spirit, which are still greatly thought of, and read with much delight by all good Christians, because they are full of good instruction and heavenly knowledge.

The son of David who succeeded him in the kingdom was called Solomon. He began to reign 1015 years before Christ was born; and it was he that built in the city of Jerusalem—which was the chief city of all the tribes of Israel—the great and glorious temple for the worship of the Lord, which was adorned with great stores of gold, and silver, and precious stones, and cedar, so as to be considered oné of the wonders of the world. All the Israelites of the twelve tribes used to come up there, according to the law of the Lord, three times in the year, for sacrifices and worship : and there was also divine service in the same place twice every day in the year, morning and evening. This temple, and the city of Jerusalem itself, was in the tribe of Judah ; and because that was the principal tribe, all the rest of the Israelites are sometimes called by the name of Jews, even to this day.

In the time of Rehoboam, son to king Solomon, who succeeded him upon the throne, ten of the twelve tribes separated from him, and set up a new king over themselves. But Judah, which was the tribe of his own family, remained under the successors of David still : so that after this there came to be two kingdoms in the land of Canaan—the kingdom of Israel, and the kingdom of Judah.

These two kingdoms lasted for many years, and had many famous kings over them. But they and their people were still continually provoking God to anger, and persecuting his prophets, and living in the practice of idolatry and other wickedness. So God gave up the kingdom of Israel first, into the hand of the enemies around, who overran and plundered the country, and kept it under their own power, and killed some of the people, and carried others into captivity.

But, even after this warning, the people of Judah continued still to follow the same sins until destruction came upon them also ; and the enemies burned their city and the temple of God, and killed many of their people, and took others into captivity into Babylon, where they remained in sorrow and hardship for many long years. At last Cyrus, king of Persia, came against Babylon, and took it. And he gave the Jews leave to return home again, and build up their temple in Jerusalem, 536 years before the birth of our Lord Jesus Christ, according as it had been foretold by the prophets of the Lord.

Chap. VII.—Of the first commencement of the Catholic Church in the Mission of the Holy Apostles, &c.

BUT even after the return from the captivity in Babylon, the Jews' country was still greatly harassed by their enemies, and one or another had power over it from time to time. And so it came to pass, that when our Saviour was born in Bethlehem,

in the land of Judah, the whole country was under
the Romans, who had their soldiers there, with a
lord-lieutenant, or governor, of their own, to keep the
people in order, and make them pay the taxes which
were imposed on them.

At this time the Romans were the greatest and
most mighty people in all the world, and almost all
other countries were in subjection to them, and governed by their authority. But, although they had
much knowledge and civilization, and more power
than all other people, they were ignorant of the true
God, and heathens like all the rest of mankind, except the Jews, at this time—practising idolatry and
superstition of all kinds ; for no one had ever yet
gone among them to preach about God, or on the
way of salvation. The Church of God before this
had been confined to the Jews, and to the land of
Canaan where they lived ; and although that was a
fat and fertile country, it was but a small place com-
pared with other conntries of the world.

But when our Blessed Saviour suffered on the cross
for all mankind, in the time of the Roman governor,
Pontius Pilate, a great change was introduced into
the world. The word and worship of the true God
was no longer confined to one people, or one small
country. But the Lord Jesus sent forth his twelve
apostles to preach in all the world, and make Christians of all nations, baptizing them in the name of
the Father, and of the Son, and of the Holy Ghost.
And they accordingly went forth, and preached every-

where the Gospel of the grace of God, in Samaria, and Antioch, and Cyprus, and Crete, and Asia, and Corinth, and Athens, and Rome, and other places. And wherever they made converts, they appointed over ·them bishops, presbyters, and deacons, with other helpers and teachers, to carry on the work of the ministry among them, and instruct them more fully in the ways of the Lord. And because these bishops and clergy were not of one particular nation, like the Jews, but out of every nation under heaven—for that reason they and the people committed to their care were called the Catholic or universal Church. This Church began first at Jerusalem, where it was founded by Christ and his twelve apostles. Next it was planted in Samaria, as we read in the book of the Acts of the Apostles ; then at Antioch, Cyprus, Iconium, Lystra, Ephesus, Corinth, Athens, Philippi, &c., and at length in the city of Rome itself.

Chap. VIII.—Of St. Patrick, the Apostle of Ireland.

THE city of Rome being, in the early days of Christianity, the head city of the whole world, the Church there soon became possessed of great influence, and the Bishops of Rome were greatly respected by the Church, especially as many of them were most holy and good men. Moreover, it was supposed that St. Peter, as well as St. Paul, had preached at Rome, and suffered martyrdom from the heathens

there; and this opinion added no small honour to
that Church and city.

Some persons have thought that Celestine, who
was Bishop of Rome in the fifth century, was the
one that we are indebted to for the conversion of Ireland; for we read in an ancient history, that, in the
year 431, Celestine sent one Palladius to be bishop
over the Christians in Ireland; but that Palladius,
after being here only two or three weeks, was driven
away by the persecution of the heathens, and went
over to Scotland, where he died shortly after. From
this it seems that there were Christians in Ireland
before that time, but perhaps not very many.

In 432, according to the common account, St.
Patrick, the principal apostle of Ireland, came over
to preach the Gospel here. Some think that Pope
Celestine sent him; and, indeed, it would have been
no great wonder if he did, considering how ready at
such good works the popes were in those days. But,
however, there is no good ancient authority for sup-
posing that he came from Celestine, and some of the
most learned in these matters think he did not, especially because none of our old Irish histories mention
anything about Celestine having sent him.

But, at all events, he preached good sound doctrine
to the people, and was the chief means, in the hand
of God, for bringing them over to the Christian faith.
We may be sure their old heathen priests, the Druids,
didn't like this much, but that they cursed and excommunicated those that would join St. Patrick and

his doctrine, or learn to read the Word of God, or listen to preaching about Christ and his salvation, that would draw them away from the religion of their forefathers. But notwithstanding all the Druids could do to keep them to the old system, the power of Christ was greater; his word prevailed—for truth never suffers by a fair inquiry—and, by the preaching of St. Patrick, the nations- of the Irish were added to the body of the Catholic Church.

It is uncertain where Patrick was born : some think in France, and some in the south of Scotland, near England. When sixteen years old, he was taken prisoner by an Irish prince, who went abroad to plunder beyond the seas. While a captive, Patrick was employed feeding pigs, near Sliev Mis, in the county of Antrim, and herding cattle there, undergoing many hardships. But his heart was softened by what he suffered, and he became very religious and fond of prayer. And after all the harsh treatment he received from the Irish in his youth, we see that afterwards, when he had his liberty, he returned them good for evil, by coming over again to preach the Gospel of the Lord.

He is said to have died in 492, aged 120 years, after having ordained very many bishops and priests throughout Ireland, and appointed the city of Armagh to be the place of the chief bishop of the whole island.

Chap. IX.—Of St. Columbkille and St. Brigid.

SHORTLY after the time of St. Patrick, there lived in Ireland great numbers of persons who were famous for their piety and zeal in the service of God. But of these none was more eminent than the famous St. Columba, or Columbkille (that is, Columb of the Churches), as he is also called, from the great number of churches founded by him.

St. Columbkille was born of a very noble family, in or about the year 521, at a place called Gartin, in Donegal, near to the town of Letterkenny. In early youth he showed great piety, and was well instructed by different clergyman of eminence, such as St. Finnian of Moville, in Down, and Cruithnecan, from whom is named the church and parish of Kilcronaghan, in Derry. Columbkille himself was the founder of the church of Derry, where a bishop was afterwards placed; and he also established many others in different parts of Ireland—one, for instance, at Durrow in the King's County, &c. When he was about forty-three years old, he left Ireland, and went over to preach the Gospel to the people of the isles and northern parts of Scotland, who were still heathens, and who were known by the name of Picts; for at that time, and for many years afterwards, the people of Ireland were called Scots; and it was some of them who went and settled in the south of Caledonia (Albania, or Pictland), and formed a kingdom there for themselves, and got possession of the country, who gave it the name of Scotland, or Scotia Minor, from their own country, which used to be called Scotia Major, *i.e.*, the Greater Scotland, as well as Hibernia, &c.

The mission of St. Columbkille among the Picts, or people of Scotland, was very successful; for he soon brought them, by his preaching and example, to embrace the faith of Christ. In his latter days he lived in the small island of Hy, or Iona, near the western coast of Scotland, in a famous monastery which he founded there. The island got from him the name of Icolmkille, or Columbkille's island, which it retains to the present day. There St. Columbkille died, when he was about seventy-seven years old, in A.D. 596 or 597. His life and miracles were written by the celebrated Adamnanus, or Eunan, Abbot of Iona, a successor of St. Columbkille's in that office, who departed this life in the year 703, and also by many others.

St. Brigid lived a little before Columbkille. She was born about the year 453, at Fochart, or Faugher, within two miles of Dundalk, in the county of Louth. Her fame for piety to God and charity to man was very great; and she was constantly labouring for the instruction and improvement of all around her. She established a famous monastery, or school of religion, at Kildare, which afterwards became the seat of a bishop's see; and her name is constantly joined with those of SS. Patrick and Columbkille, as being all together the three most famous among the ancient saints of Ireland.

Chap. X.—*Of St. Columbanus, and various other eminent men of the ancient Irish.*

A.D. 600, &c.

BESIDES the celebrated saints whom we have already mentioned, there are on record in history the names of others without number, who flourished in the days of Patrick and Columbkille, and afterwards—such as St. Columbanus of Luxeu and Bobio; St. Finnian of Clonard, in Meath; St. Kieran of Clonmacnoise, and St. Kieran of Saigir; St. Brendan of Birr, and St. Brendan of Clonfert; St. Kevin of Glendalough; St. Comgall of Bangor; St. Canice of Kilkenny, &c. &c.; Aidan, Finan, Colman, &c.

These persons were mostly abbots, and heads of monastic schools or colleges, into which they gathered very large numbers of monks and pupils, and took much pains in instructing them in religious and common knowledge. They taught them in particular, young and old, to read the Bible, and especially the book of psalms, and to sing the praises of God. And they trained up great numbers of young persons to be clergymen and ministers of the Church;

They also taught those who were under them to till the ground well, and to be very industrious—to be content with little food and sleep, and humble clothing, and never to eat the bread of idleness. They found it a great help and comfort for so many people to be living together, and assisting one another, when there was much warring and fighting, and few or no large towns for people to live together in.

One of the most famous of those whom we have mentioned in this chapter, was Columbanus of Bobio. He was born somewhere in Leinster about A.D. 550, and was remarkable in very early youth for his great piety and singular knowledge of the word of God. Being anxious to do good abroad in some foreign parts beyond the seas, he went to France, and settled there at a place called Luxeu, where he founded a famous monastic school, and laboured much for the benefit of the people in the neighbourhood. But the King of Burgundy, in which Luxeu was situated, was angry with Columbanus (because he reproved him for his sinful and immoral life), and obliged him to leave that country, much to his regret and sorrow, after he had been twenty years living there. He then removed to the north of Italy, and settled among the Lombards, whose king was kind and friendly to him ; and here he founded another famous monastery at a place called Bobio, where he lived afterwards to the time of his death, which took place in A.D. 615.

Great numbers of the disciples of Columbanus

became famous afterwards in France and elsewhere,
and were appointed to bishoprics, and other high
offices.   Also vast numbers of others from Ireland
went and settled in various parts of Germany, France,
Italy, and other places, many of whom, in like
manner, became famous as bishops, abbots, heads
of schools and colleges, and eminent in other ways ;
so that we need not wonder that in those days Ireland came to enjoy a great renown and fame for
learning throughout all the countries of Europe, for
theology, music, astronomy, copying of manuscripts,
and ornamenting them, and such other arts and
branches of philosophy as were then most esteemed
and cultivated.   So that to the present day, not only
in England and Scotland, but in all parts of Europe,
there are traces to be found, more or less, of those
famous Irishmen of the olden time ; and abbeys, and
cathedral churches, and towns and cities, are still
called after their names, and exist as monuments to
their memories.   Such were St. Gall, of Switzerland ;
St. Dichuil, of Lure, in France ; St. Furseus, of
Lagny, near Paris ; St. Kilian, of Wurtzburgh ; St.
Maidulf, of Malmesbury, in England ; St. Virgil, of
Saltzburgh ; and others, too numerous to be mentioned in this place.

Chap. XI.—*Of St. Aidan's preaching to the Saxons, &c.*

AT the time when St. Patrick came over to preach the gospel in Ireland, the country now called England was inhabited by the people called Britons, who had some knowledge of Christianity among them, and bishops and clergy of their own to look after them, as all the other churches of the world had. But the heathen Saxons came shortly after from beyond sea, and invaded the Britons, and took their land for themselves, persecuting and oppressing Christianity in particular. And they drove most of the Britons into Wales for shelter, and founded seven kingdoms for themselves in the rest of the country, which made up what was called the Heptarchy. By this means the greater part of England became a Pagan country once more, excepting Wales, where the British Christians abode. These British Christians in Wales afterwards kept up a great intercourse with the people of Ireland, and they were both constantly going backwards and forwards from the one country to the other—Britons coming over to get instruction in this island, and sometimes to give it also; and Irishmen, in like manner, going across to Wales, and establishing schools, and giving instruction to the people there, and sometimes learning too, from such teachers as had a great name in Britain, as St. David, and Gildas, Cadoc, and others.

The names of the seven kingdoms founded by the Saxons were these—1, Kent ; 2, the South Saxons ; 3, the West Saxons ; 4, the East Saxons ; 5, Northumberland ; 6, the East Angles ; 7, Mercia. Now Gregory the Great, Bishop of Rome, sent over a missionary named Augustine, and some others, in A.D. 596, from Rome, to preach the gospel to the Pagan Saxons in England ; and they began at Kent, which was the most southern part, and after the conversion of the king there, continued their work with no small success. But a far larger and more important portion of the same work was performed by the Irish monks of St. Columbkille's monastery in Iona, who were permitted, in the providence of God, to be the principal instruments in this great undertaking.

Oswald, King of Northumberland in A. D. 633, was a Christian prince, and had been educated by Irish instructors from Scotland. On coming to the throne, he was very anxious to have the gospel preached to his subjects, that they might become Christians ; and, accordingly, he sent word to those that had instructed himself, to send him some preachers of the gospel. And he got from them a very good and pious man, by name Aidan, a monk of the college of Iona, whom they ordained a bishop, and sent to preach to the Saxons of Northumberland. But Aidan did not understand the Saxon tongue, and the Saxons could not understand Aidan's Irish sermons ; so King Oswald, who could speak both languages, was good enough to explain Bishop

Aidan's discourses to the people. And the labours of Aidan, and the other Irish teachers who followed him into England, were very successful, so that in a short time the people in general throughout the large kingdom of Northumberland, came to profess the Christian faith once more; for they had indeed already been nominally converted by some of the Roman missionaries from Kent, but could not have been very well instructed by them, since before the reign of King Oswald, they had all gone back to paganism again.

Chap XII.—*Of the Paschal Controversy between the Church of Rome and the Ancient Irish, &c.*

AIDAN was bishop of Northumberland for seventeen years, and was greatly beloved and honoured by all the people of that country for his piety and goodness, and his kind and gentle disposition. He died in A.D. 651, and was succeeded by another Irishman from Iona, named Finan. This Finan also was greatly liked by the people, and lived among them as their bishop for ten years. And when he died, in A.D. 651, another Irishman from Iona named Colman was appointed bishop of the same see.

In the time of Bishop Colman, there arose a very serious quarrel between him and his Irish fellow-labourers, on the one side, and the Church of Rome and her missionaries on the other side. The quarrel was one that had begun between the Irish and the Church of Rome some time before, but it did not come to a regular head until the days of Bishop Colman. It was, as we shall see, about a rather trifling matter.

When Augustine came to preach to the Saxons, the Church of Rome used to reckon the time of keeping Easter in one way, and the Irish people in another way, as they had learned from their old pastors and teachers, and so, as they did not agree about the time, the Irish Easter would sometimes happen a month, perhaps, before, or after the Roman festival, and each party supported its own system with great bitterness; so that when Bishop Daganus, an Irishman, was over in England, about the year 608, he would not eat meat in the same lodging with Laurentius, archbishop of Canterbury, on account of his belonging to the Church of Rome. The Britons agreed with the Irish in this matter; and any one of their party that would adopt the Roman customs, they called a heretic. The Romans, on the other hand, said that they followed the system of the Catholic Church, and that the Irish, and Picts, and Britons, had no right to be setting themselves up against the practice of the whole world. There was some difference amongst them about the tonsure, or mode of trimming the monks' hair, and also about baptism, but that about Easter was the principal point in dispute. For these disputes, the two parties would refuse to meet each other in company, or even at prayers in Church, or to salute one another in a friendly way upon the road. In fact they would have no more intercourse with one another than with pagans. And no people stood up more obstinately for the Irish customs than the followers of Columbkille, and such of the people as were under their influence.

Chap. XIII.—*How the Matter was discussed and settled in the Synod of Whitby.*

A.D. 664.

NOW the followers of the Roman missionaries in England were much annoyed to find the Irish bishops and teachers, whom they looked upon as no Catholics, exercising so much influence, and extending their system so much in that country. And so they prevailed upon Oswy, king of Northumberland, and his son Alchfrid, to call a synod or council at a place called Whitby, in order to make a general rule on the subject for the whole country, and put an end to all disputing about the matter. The principal instrument of the Roman party was a learned Saxon priest named Wilfrid, tutor to the king's son Alfrid, who had been partly educated at Rome, and was greatly attached to the church there, but had a great contempt for the "schismatics of Britain and Ireland," and the corrupt system with which they were "poisoning" the minds of the people in England; for that was the light in which this Wilfrid regarded the Christians of Britain and Ireland, and their religious practices.

The council of Whitby accordingly met in the year 664. And when they came together, St. Colman, who was to defend the Irish system, was allowed to speak first, and show what he had to say for himself; when he spoke as follows :—" This Easter that I observe is what I have received from those that were over me, who sent me to be bishop in this place; which all our fathers, men beloved of God, are well known to have celebrated according to the same plan. And will any one venture to slight or object to it, when it is the same that the B. Evangelist St. John, the disciple specially beloved of the Lord, and all the churches under his care did follow. Or is it to be supposed that St. Columbkille and his successors, men beloved of God, who observed Easter in the same manner that we do, did believe in or follow what was contrary to the Holy Scriptures ?"

But Wilfrid told Colman in reply, that it was a foolish thing for him and his followers to be fighting against the whole world : and that if Columbkille was ever so great and holy, still he was not as great as St. Peter : for that he was prince of the Apostles, and that the Lord had said to him, "Thou art Peter, and upon this rock I will build my church, and the gates of hell shall not prevail against it, and I will give unto thee the keys of the kingdom of heaven :" and that any one who followed the Irish Easter should be under a curse thereby.

So King Oswy asked Colman was it true that
Christ had given such a promise to St. Peter, and
Colman allowed that it was. "Oh! then," said the
king, with a smile on his face, "if that be so, I must
not go against St. Peter, for fear that when I'd come
to the gate of the kingdom of heaven, there would be
no person to open, if I were to anger him that is allowed to have the keys." And so a law was made
that the Roman system should prevail, and the Irish
be done away for ever.

But Colman was greatly displeased at this result.
And seeing that his doctrine was despised, and his
sect, as they called it, looked down upon, he gave up
his bishopric and all his influence there, rather than
give in to the Roman rites, and be subject to their authority, and all the Irish that were under him came
away at the same time, and many of the English
monks also, who chose to continue to the Irish system ; and they settled in the county Mayo, in the pro-
vince of Connaught, and lived there. In making this
choice to leave England, Colman was partly influenced, it is said, by fear of the displeasure of his
countrymen, in case he should remain in Northumberland, and give in to the ways and influence of the
Church of Rome. Wilfrid became bishop in his
place in England, and was always a great upholder
of the Church of Rome. "He was," says Bede,
"the first bishop of the English race that introduced
the Catholic way of living into the churches of that
country."

Chap. XIV.—Of the love of the ancient Irish for the study of the Holy Scriptures.

THE fame of Ireland in those days for knowledge of divinity and other learning was so great, that large numbers of people came from England and from foreign parts to receive their education in this country, so that the Church History of our island abounds with such examples.

It was their knowledge and study of the Word of God in particular that gained for the saints of Ireland so high a reputation. Of St. Patrick it is said by his nephew, St. Seachlin, that he "found a sacred treasure in the Sacred Volume;" and the monk Joceline, who wrote his life, says that he would spend days and nights in expounding the Scriptures to the people. St. Columbkille also was very fond of the Scriptures, and of the Psalms in particular, which he was writing out at the time of his death. And Bede says of him and his successors, that they practised only "such works of piety and chastity as they could learn in the writings of the prophets, evangelists, and apostles"—*i.e.,* in the Bible. In the life of St. Brigid, we are told that she took great pleasure in hearing the reading, and preaching, and expounding of the Word of God: and that she would not take her food any morning until her soul had been refreshed with its food, in the Word of God—as St. Peter says, "Desire the sincere milk of the Word, that ye may grow thereby." And Cogitosus, who wrote another life of St. Brigid, says, that it was her custom to "scatter among all around her the most wholesome seed of the Word of God." In like manner, Bede says of the good St. Aidan, that it was the daily work of himself and all his followers, both monks and laity, "to be occupied either in reading the Scriptures, or learning the Psalms." St. Columbanus also, when he was a young boy, was put to study under a teacher named Senile, who had a great name for knowledge of the Scriptures, and he instructed his pupil carefully "in the whole" of them, so that while yet very young, he wrote, as we are told, a very interesting explanation of the Book of Psalms.

So Dr. Lanigan, in his learned "Church History of Ireland," remarks, that St. Finnian, of Clonard, was "distinguished for his extraordinary learning and knowledge of the holy Scriptures;" and that St. Carthagh went to France, and "spent some years in the practice of a penitential life, and in the study of the holy Scriptures;" and that St. Gall, for "his superior knowledge of the holy Scriptures," and other good qualities, was offered the bishopric of the city of Constance, in Switzerland. And in the legends of St. Kieran of Saigir, we read that this saint, in his old age, was still "very humble in every way, loving much to hear and read the holy Scriptures, even till he became weak from age; for it is reported of him,

that he, with other saints of Ireland of that time,
went in his old age to St. Finnian, Abbot of Clonard,
who had a great name for wisdom, and used to read
at his holy school in the divine Scriptures." Such
are the words of the legends of St. Kieran on this
point.

*Chap. XV.—How the English and
   other foreigners used to come to
   study and be educated in Ireland.*

NOW as to the English and others from abroad,
who came over to be educated in Ireland in
those times, they were very many, and some of them
very famous. A few of them may properly be mentioned in this place.

And first we may read, as Dr. Lanigan observes,
in the life of St. Senan of Inniscatthy, that when he
was at Iniscarra, near Cork, about the year 530, " a
vessel arrived in Cork harbour, bringing fifty religious
persons, passengers from the Continent, who came
to Ireland, either for the purpose of leading a life of
stricter discipline, or of improving themselves in the
study of the Scriptures"—" a study then much cultivated in Ireland." Gildas the Briton also studied
for some time in Ireland, about A.D. 510, and became " eminently qualified for preaching the Word
of God," as Dr. Lanigan also notes. So, according
to the same authority, St. Petrock, of Padstow, in
Cornwall, left his own country in the sixth century,

and came over and "spent twenty years in Ireland,
applying himself to the study of the Scriptures, and
to the acquirement of general knowledge."

But still more interesting is what we read in Bede
relative to the same point, in the following passage :—
"There were," says he, "in Ireland at this time, numbers of the nobility, and also of the middling sort of
the English people, who left home, in the time of the
bishops Colman and Finan, and went over there, either
to study the Word of God, or else to lead a stricter
life. Some went into the monasteries, and others
lived by themselves, and visited their various tutors,
and received lessons from them. And the people of
Ireland gave them all a hearty welcome, and supplied
them with food without any charge, and provided
them also with books to learn out of, and instruction
besides, all entirely free of cost." So ready were the
Irish to be kind and friendly to the young people of
England in those days.

Among others who were educated by the Irish people in this age, were Edilwin, who became eminent as
Bishop of Lindis, in England ; Agilbert, Bishop of the
West Saxons, and afterwards Bishop of Paris, who
spent, as Bede says, "no small time in Ireland, for
the purpose of reading the Scriptures ;" Alfrid, King
of Northumberland, who was, according to Bede, "a
man most learned in the Scriptures ;" the celebrated
Saxon priest, Egbert, who lived, as the same author
states, in Ireland for a long time, "in prayers, and
continence, and meditation on the Holy Scriptures,"

in which he became very deeply learned ; Willibrord,
the celebrated Saxon missionary, who became afterwards Archbishop of Utrecht ; and hundreds besides,
whose names, alas ! may find no place in this little
history.

Chap. XVI.—About the Danish In-vasions, Brian Boru, &c.

A.D. 795–1013.

ABOUT the year of our Lord 800, the Pagan
Danes, or Nortmans, began to invade Ireland ;
and they spoiled and wasted all before them whither-
soever they came—slaughtering the clergy, burning
the colleges and monasteries, destroying the books,
and plundering the property ; for the people of Ireland were too weak, and too much divided into provinces and parties, to be able to withstand these enemies.   They sometimes, indeed, gained victories over
them, but it signified little ; for when hundreds of
them were killed, hundreds more would come over
from abroad to fill up their places.   One of the worst
of them was Turgesius, who came over from Norway
about the year 815, with a great army, and took the
title of King of Ireland for thirty years.   At the
end of this time he was taken by Maelseachlin, chief
monarch of Ireland, and drowned in Loch Var, in
Meath.   These cruel tyrants, however, still carried
on their depredations and wars, driving away learning
and civilization out of the country, and forcing the

most of those who cared for such things to take refuge in foreign parts, while their native land, in the
meantime, was ruined with blood and slaughter ; and
the Irish people, in the course of two hundred years,
were left little better in religion or learning than those
who invaded them.   At length Brian Boru, King of
Munster, gave them a great beating at Clontarf, near
Dublin, on Good Friday, in the year 1013.   Brian
himself was killed in that battle, and his son Morogh,
and grandson Turlogh, and many other Irish princes
and nobles.   But the Danish army was entirely rout-
ed and scattered, and they were never able to give
so much trouble in Ireland again.   Brian was a valiant and brave king, and good to his subjects ; but
he did what was wrong in seizing for himself, by a
strong hand, the chief monarchy of Ireland, which
belonged not to him, but to another — an act
which led to much fighting and trouble in Ireland
afterwards.

Of the Irish people who lived at home in the
Danish times, the most famous was Cormac Mac-
Cuillenan, King and Bishop of Cashel, celebrated for
writing books and fighting battles.   He was the author of the famous *Psalter of Cashel,* and also of
Cormac's Glossary of Irish words.   He died in battle, in A.D. 908.   Another very eminent Irish writer
of the same century, who seems to have lived at
home, was the commentator Sedulius, who composed
very useful notes on the Epistles of the Apostle St.
Paul.

D

practice gave no small offence to the bishops of Ireland, and particularly to the successor of St. Patrick at Armagh. Nor need we wonder that they were displeased at seeing their authority interfered with by a foreign influence in that way. This very interference helped also, after a while, to bring the power of the Church of Rome into this country. But of this we shall speak more at large in what follows.

Chap. XVIII.—Concerning the Independence of the ancient Irish Church.

FIRST, however, let us observe, that before the time of which we now speak, the Church of Rome had no power nor supremacy whatsoever in Ireland, any more than the Church of Jerusalem, or Antioch, or Alexandria, or any other foreign church. So far were the Irish from having any such opinion of the power of the Pope or Church of Rome in Columbkille's days, that the learned Cardinal Baronius, in his famous "Ecclesiastical Annals," says, that at that time the bishops of Ireland were all schismatics, separated from the communion of the Church of Rome, and in close league with her enemies. Be that as it may, however, the Irish were ready enough, as we know, to quarrel with the Romans in those days, and separate from their communion, for very trifling matters, although they did not think them trifling, but supposed Rome and her followers to be in great error in regard to them.

At all events, it appears certain that for 700 years after St. Patrick's arrival in Ireland in 432, no Pope ever nominated, confirmed, sanctioned, or appointed, in any way, any one bishop, or archbishop, or other dignitary, for any one see in Ireland; or gave a charter to any college, or school, or professor, or a license or dispensation of any kind for Ireland; or heard one cause connected with the church of this country; or had the least hand in the canonizing or blessing, or appointing of any single one of the ancient saints of Ireland, who lived before the twelfth century; or was allowed in any other way to interfere with the concerns of the church of this island, until that time, *i. e.*, 1132.

In short, the method pursued by these ancient Irishmen, whenever they wanted a new bishop, was for the prince, and prelates, and clergy, and people, of the district, some or all, to select one for themselves, choosing whomsoever they might think most fit, without any application to Rome for leave or license, authority or sanction; and whomsoever they chose in this way, they had him ordained bishop at home by some of their own bishops, without any regard to what might be the practice of any foreign church in such cases. And in like manner the Irish prelates appointed new bishoprics and archbishoprics as they thought fit, by their own proper authority. And even the people of the Danish cities in Ireland acted pretty much after the same manner, only they, as we have already seen, used to send their bishops elect across the water, to be consecrated by the Archbishops of Canterbury, who acknowledged at this time the doctrine of the supremacy of the Popes of Rome.

Chap. XIX.—*Of Gille, Bishop of the Danes of Limerick, the first Pope's Legate for all Ireland.*

NOW, about the beginning of the twelfth century, or in the year 1106, the people of the Danish city of Limerick had for their bishop a very famous individual, named Gille or Gillebert, who is also the first bishop of Limerick recorded in our histories. What country Gille belonged to we are not told; this, however, we know for certain, that he had studied in Normandy in his early days, and had acquired among the Normans there a great fondness for the discipline, ritual practices, and general system of the Church of Rome; and when he became bishop in Ireland, he did all in his power to extend the same system in this country, and kept up also a correspondence with his friend Anselm, Archbishop of Canterbury, who had become acquainted with Gillebert abroad, and who encouraged him afterwards in his proceedings, as bishop, at Limerick.

Before the time of Gille, the Roman mass had not come into use in Ireland; but the clergy and people followed their own ancient forms of prayer, which

had been given them by the old saints of the country.
And so some followed one form, or order, or use, as
it was called, and some followed another. Gille was
greatly scandalized at this, and did all he could to
get these forms done away, and the Roman one
brought in in their stead. And when he brought
the matter before the bishops of Ireland, several of
them asked him to write a book on the subject,
explaining his views and method in regard to it;
and Gille did so, and wrote such a book, containing
the Roman order of service for their use. In the
preface, he complained that "almost all Ireland was
led astray by those different and schismatical orders,"
or forms of service that they used, and that it would
be far better for the people to have "one Catholic
and Roman office" for their worship. And so it
appears that from this time forward, the Roman form
began to be more and more used, until it came to
prevail generally in Ireland. Gille also wrote, for
the people of Ireland, a treatise on the different
orders of the clergy, teaching them of the nature and
authority of the Pope's office, and telling them that
he was Head of the Church all over the world, and
Vicar of Christ, &c., and explaining the offices of
other ranks and orders of the clergy also. Gillebert
"signalized his zeal," says Dr. Lanigan, " by en-
deavouring to bring all the practices, liturgical, and
connected with the church service, of which there
was a great variety in Ireland, to one uniform system,
conformable to that of the particular Church of

Rome." For these services, Gille was made Pope's
legate for all Ireland, being, as St. Bernard tells us,
the first person that ever held such an office in this
country. It seems likely that it was Anselm got him
the office; for though Ireland was not yet under the
English kings, still the bishops of the Danish cities
had been placed under the English primates, which
naturally led the governors of England, in church
and state, to begin to take an interest in the affairs of
our island.

Chap. XX.—Of the Old Religion of Ireland before Gille's time.

BUT, we may ask, what did the people think of
Gille, and his plans for church reform, and
for bringing in the power and authority of the Popes
into Ireland?—or did they readily agree to his
notions, after having, in former ages, maintained so
hot a quarrel with the Church of Rome about Easter,
and other matters, and shown so little regard to her
laws? In answer to this we must observe, that the
people now were not generally, like those of old, so
religious or well-informed as to take much interest in
these matters. Wars and plunder, instead of books
and learning, had occupied their minds for three
hundred years; and it is no great wonder if, at the
end of that time, the people at large knew more
about storming a Danish garrison, or plundering a
monastery, or building a rath for their own defence,

than about the history and religion of their forefathers, or of other countries of the world in their
own time.

The form of Christianity received among the ancient Irish of the earlier times, was of a pure and
simple character in most of its features. Some par-
ticulars connected with it have come under our notice
already, as, for instance, that they were entirely free
from any subjection or obedience to the Pope of
Rome. They had also great numbers of bishops,
and appointed them wherever they chose, without
any application to him. They respected Jerusalem
as the mother-church of the whole world, and did
not regard the Church of Rome as having any title
to be the mistress of all churches. An Irishman
would give up a bishopric sooner than give in to that,
as we have seen already. The Holy Scriptures they
loved and valued above all books, and made them
their great rule and guide in matters of faith and
practice; appealing to them in their controversies
and writings, and establishing none of their doctrines upon tradition, or the unanimous consent of
the Fathers. And even after all the ravages of the
Danes, we find Sulgen, who was appointed Bishop of
St. David's, about 1070, coming to study in Ireland,
as a place famous for learning of the word of God,
and spending many years here in the study of the
Scriptures. Nor did the old Irish, in the days of
Patrick and Columbkille, or Colman and Aidan,
know anything about the infallibility of the Pope or

Church of Rome, or about purgatory, nor did they invoke nor pray to saints or angels. As to the giving of the cup to the laity, Dr. Lanigan's own statement is, that "It is not denied that in old times it was practised in Ireland, as well as everywhere else." "The marriage of the clergy," says Mr. Thomas Moore, another Roman Catholic author, in his "History of Ireland," "though certainly not approved of, was yet permitted and practised among the first Irish Christians." In the life of St. Patrick himself, there appears to be evidence of this, for his father, as he himself tells us, was a deacon, and his grandfather a priest.

As for the Holy Communion of the Lord's Supper, the ancient Irish before these times believed, as does the Reformed Church at this day, that the body and blood of Christ are verily and indeed taken and received by the faithful in that ordinance. But yet they did not hold the doctrine of transubstantiation. Indeed Mr. Moore himself seems to speak with much reason and moderation on this matter; for he appears to acknowledge plainly that there was as least some degree of error in "the doctrine" which he says was "put forth then recently by Paschasius Radbert, who maintained that the body present in the Eucharist was the same carnal and palpable body which was born of the Virgin, which suffered on the cross, and rose from the dead; whereas the belief of the Catholic Church," says he, "on this point of doctrine, has always been, that the body of Christ is under the symbols not corporeally or carnally, but in a spiritual manner." So speaks Mr. Moore on this head; nor is it likely the old Irish would very widely disagree with his doctrine as here stated. •

Chap. XXI.—*State of Religion in Ireland at the commencement of the Danish wars, and afterwards.*

ALTHOUGH the early saints of Ireland used not the Roman mass-book in their devotions, still the prayers of their own which they did use in the churches appear to have been in the Latin tongue, which was, probably, because that was the language best known to their earliest Christian teachers, and the one which was then in general use throughout Europe, and, perhaps, coming into more general use in Ireland, as English now is. This was one of the few things to be regretted in the religious system of the first Christian teachers of Ireland.

But more serious errors crept in in the course of time. Among others, prayers for the dead began to be used very early, although at first they used to pray more especially for the saints that were entered into rest, and so *for* the Virgin Mary herself, by name; so little did they think of praying *to* her. Nor are we told in the ancient lives of Patrick, Columbkille, Brigid, or Columbanus, or any other of those old worthies, that one of them ever prayed to or for her, or any other person departed this life.

From the writings of Ængus Ceile De, however, who lived about 790, it would seem that prayers to dead men were then becoming very common in Ireland; for Ængus uses many such prayers to various monks and saints that were buried in different parts of Ireland. Such a departure from the simple faith once delivered to the saints, was surely sufficient to draw down the anger of God on this country, in the terrible visitation of the Danish wars, which began so soon after. These wars left the people, in the time of Gille, very ignorant and careless about religion, without much knowledge or concern about the doctrines of the Church of Rome, whether they were true or false, or useless for themselves to adopt or not, at least so far as they had not of themselves adopted similar doctrines already.

When Gille, therefore, and others who were most in earnest about religion, and had more knowledge, began to form plans for improving such a people as this, they would have no great difficulty in getting any of them who were willing to be taught, to follow whatsoever system they would recommend to them; and accordingly the Church of Rome began, by degrees, to have many strong friends and supporters in this country. Of those who followed Gillebert in this way, by far the most active and famous was the celebrated St. Malachy, Archbishop of Armagh, of whom we shall have occasion to say more in the next chapter.

Chap. XXII.—*Of Malachy O'Morgair, commonly called St. Malachy.*

ÆLMOEDOC O'Morgair, commonly known in our Church Annals by the name of St. Malachy, was born of an ancient and noble family, about the year 1095. For his singular talents and piety he was ordained before the regular appointed time, and presently made vicar to Celsus, the primate of Armagh. St. Bernard, who wrote his life, tells us that when appointed to this office, "he busied himself in establishing in all the churches of his district the apostolical constitutions and the decrees of the holy fathers, and in particular the customs of the holy Church of Rome." He also brought into the same churches, as the same author informs us, the custom of chaunting and singing the canonical hours, which, though common in other parts of the world, was not then used in Armagh itself; and he also, according to the same authority, " restored the practice of confession, the use of the sacrament of confirmation, and the marriage contract, all of which," says he, "were unknown to the people, or else neglected by them;" which seems to mean partly that they did not follow the customs of the Church of Rome in regard to them; for they certainly could not be quite ignorant of them. In his plans for improvement, Malachy would not go entirely upon his own judgment, but was guided partly by the counsels of other friends, who knew more about the customs of the foreign Churches than he did, particularly his friend Gille, of whom we have already spoken, and whose book he no doubt studied carefully; and Malchus, Bishop of Lismore, with whom he also studied. This Malchus had been a monk of Winchester, in England.

When about thirty years old, Malachy was made Bishop of Connor—a bishopric, says Bernard, where he soon found that "it was not men but brutes he had to deal with. Such a set of ill-mannered, ungodly, stiffnecked, filthy, barbarians, he had never met before; with the name of Christians, but in reality Pagans—people who paid no tithes, nor first-fruits, nor cared for lawful wedlock, nor about going to confession. In fact, no one there would impose a penance, nor submit to it." Malachy, however, wrought hard among them, and with such success, that Bernard says that he soon got the old "barbarous customs abolished, and those of Rome introduced in their stead."

Chap. XXIII.—How Malachy was appointed Primate, and how he promoted foreign influence in Ireland.

CELSUS, Archbishop of Armagh, dying in 1129, appointed in his will that Malachy should succeed him as Primate of Ireland; and Malachy ac-

cordingly held that office for three years; but afterwards resigned it, and became Bishop of Down, having first selected one Gelasius to succeed him as
primate in Armagh.

He himself was still carrying on his plans for the
improvement of the Church of Ireland, and uniting
it completely to the Church of Rome. But he began
to think, according to the doctrine contained in Gille's
book about the authority of the Pope, that it was not
right of himself to be making so many changes without applying to him for his licence and sanction; and
he therefore determined to go to Rome, and consult
his holiness about these matters. He was also hoping to get from him, for the archbishops of Armagh
and Cashel, the use of the pall—a kind of honorary
ornament which the popes used to send to archbishops of their communion, but which had never yet
been received nor worn by any Irish primate. The
people of Ireland were not quite satisfied with Malachy's undertaking this journey; but he was resolved
on going, and therefore started · accordingly, and
came to Rome in 1139.

Pope Innocent II. was highly pleased and inter-
ested at seeing such an unusual thing as a bishop
from Ireland coming to consult him, and he therefore treated Malachy with great kindness; had several conversations with him during the month he spent
in Rome, and asked him a great many questions
about the state of Ireland, the habits of the people,
the condition of the churches, and other things of the

same kind.   And then, as Bishop Gille was now getting old and unequal to his duties, the Pope appointed
Malachy, when he was returning home to Ireland, to
succeed him in the office of legate for all Ireland.
The palls, however, were not yet given, as the Pope
doubted perhaps whether they would yet be generally
acceptable.

Malachy, while abroad, becoming acquainted with
foreign monks, thought that such as they would be
very useful in Ireland, and accordingly brought over
some of those called Cistercians with him from France
to Ireland ; and afterwards sent over other persons
from Ireland to learn their system, and extend it in
this country.   Institutions of the kind were afterwards a great means of promoting foreign influence
in Ireland.

A few years after, in 1148, Malachy set out again
to visit the Pope, and ask for the palls once more.
He was however overtaken by a fever on the way,
which brought his days to an end in France, before
he had gained the object of his wishes.   He was afterwards canonized by Pope Clement about the year
1190, and was the first Irishman who was named a
saint by the authority of the Church of Rome.

Chap. *XXIV.*—*The Pope gives Henry II. leave to invade Ireland.*

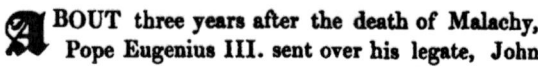 BOUT three years after the death of Malachy,
Pope Eugenius III. sent over his legate, John

Paparo, into this country with palls for the Irish archbishops. Paparo held a Synod at Kells, in the year 1152, and brought in different laws for the government of the Irish Church; as that there should be four archbishops in Ireland, wearing palls—viz., two new ones, Dublin and Tuam, besides Armagh and Cashel, that existed already: also that the clergy should not be allowed to marry; that the people should all pay tithes, &c. &c. This synod was plainly a new step towards extending the Pope's authority into Ireland.

A few years more, however, brought on circumstances of still greater importance in connexion with this matter. For in the year 1154, Henry II. became King of England, and another person of English origin became Pope of Rome, by the name of Adrian the Fourth; and by an arrangement made between these two, Ireland became completely subject at once to the spiritual supremacy of Rome, and at the same time to the temporal dominion of the kings of England.

Henry II., the Norman Prince of England, being a warlike and ambitious monarch, was resolved on adding Ireland, if possible, to his dominions. For his people, the Normans, had now gotten possession of everything in England and Wales, and they were anxious to be seizing more of what was not their own. And as William the Conqueror came to invade and seize upon England with the blessing of the Pope to back his efforts in the cause, Henry II. thought that he might probably make an attempt upon Ireland, with similar advantages.

Pope Adrian had a very particular friend, a bishop, named John of Salisbury, who was also very intimate and friendly with King Henry II. And so Henry got this John to apply to the Pope for permission to come and invade Ireland, with his good-will and blessing. He knew most probably how the influence of the Church of Rome was increasing in Ireland, and he considered that, by forming an alliance with such a power, he might easily carry out his own designs upon the island which he coveted. He therefore promised the Pope that, in return for his good-will and assistance in this matter, he would pay him an annual tax out of Ireland, and do all in his power in favour of the rights of the church there. So the Pope readily agreed to his proposal, and sent him a very kind letter granting him all his desire : and he also sent him, by John of Salisbury, a splendid ring of emerald set in gold, as a token of the power he gave him to govern Ireland ; which ring was afterwards carefully preserved among the royal treasures.

Chap. XXV.—The Bull of Pope Adrian.

THE letter or bull which Pope Adrian sent to King Henry has been preserved in many records, and is to the following effect :—

" Adrian Bishop, servant of the servants of God,

to our well-beloved son in Christ, the illustrious King
of the English, health and apostolical benediction :

"Your majesty is desirous of engaging in a noble
and useful undertaking; an undertaking that will get
you a glorious renown on earth, and be the means of
increasing your happiness in heaven hereafter, when
you turn your thoughts, like a true Catholic prince,
to the object of widening the borders of the church,
and explaining the true Christian faith to an ignorant
and uncivilized people, so as to root out from among
them the vicious practices that are growing, like bad
weeds, in that part of the Lord's vineyard.

"With this object in view, you are anxious to have
the benefit of our apostolic advice and countenance.
So proper a mode of proceeding will, we trust, with
the Lord's permission, be crowned with an abundant
measure of success.

"Certainly there can be no doubt but that Ireland,
and all other islands where Christ the Sun of Righ-
teousness hath shined, and where the Gospel has
been preached, do belong by right to St. Peter,
and the Holy Roman Church, as your majesty also
allows. For which reason we are anxious in our
conscience to provide for them right instruction in
the way of godliness.

"You have expressed to us, well-beloved son in
the Lord, your wish to undertake an expedition to
Ireland, in order to bring the people there into
subjection to right laws, and to banish the vicious
practices which abound there. And you say that you

are willing to pay to St. Peter a yearly tribute of one penny for every house there, and to maintain the rights and privileges of the church in that country.

"So pious and laudable a desire we cannot but regard with such favourable feelings as it deserves; nor can we refuse to agree to the petition you have addressed to us. And we therefore express hereby our will and pleasure, that in order to widen the bounds of the church—to check the evil practices that abound there—to improve the people's morals, and instruct them in the paths of virtue—in short, for the purpose of advancing the Christian religion in general—you should proceed to that island, and there do whatever shall be for the honour of God, and the welfare of the country.

"And let the people of that land receive you in honourable style, and respect you as their lord, provided always that the rights of the church be secured and maintained, and the yearly penny for each house be duly paid to St. Peter and the Holy Roman Church.

"If, then, you will carry out this plan which you have thought of, be careful to use your exertions for the improvement of that people in good manners. And let your agents and helpers there too be persons of sound faith and good character. So as that the church may be had in honour there, the Christian religion take root and flourish, and everything pertaining to the honour of God and the salvation of souls be settled by you in such a way as to increase

your prize of bliss from God in eternity, and secure
you on earth a name of glory to all generations."

Chap. XXVI.—What the Irish thought of the Bull, and what Dermod Mac Morogh was doing about this time.

BUT here again, what did the people of Ireland
or their clergy think of this new proceeding on
the part of the Pope? Were they willing to obey
this bull of Adrian's, and to receive "the illustrious
king of the English" as their lord and ruler?

The people probably did not care much about the
matter. They had already five kingdoms at least
among themselves, namely, Leinster, Ulster, Meath,
Connaught, and Munster; or even more, by occasional subdivisions of these. And of the five kings
it would happen, that sometimes one, sometimes
another, would be regarded as chief monarch; so
that it did not seem any great hardship to be under
a new chief monarch in England, especially so great
and famous a name as Henry II. Indeed it is not
unlikely that the princes and people of Ireland may
have hoped for good from Henry's being over them,
and expected that it would help to promote the peace
and improvement of the country.

But as for the Pope's bidding, most of them cared
too little about the Church of Rome, or indeed about
any sort of religion at this time, to be much influenced
one way or the other, as far as themselves were con-

cerned, by such a consideration. But those of the
Irish bishops and clergy who were walking in the
steps of Gillebert and Malachy—and they were now
many and influential—would of course be glad to
obey the Pope's bull themselves, and encourage all
that were under their influence to act in like manner.

But, however, at all events, King Henry, after
getting this Bull, in A.D. 1155, was for many years
too much occupied to come and invade Ireland, as the
Pope had allowed him to do, until at length some circumstances happened in Ireland itself, which greatly
favoured his desire to have this country brought under his own dominion.

Dermod Mac Morogh, king of Leinster, a violent
and bad prince, had invaded, in 1153, the territories
of Tiernan O'Ruarc, prince of Braiffny, and carried
off Tiernan's wife Dervorgal, whom he brought with
him into Leinster. This act of wickedness involved
him in trouble and wars for many years after; the
end of which was, that at length, in A.D. 1167, he
was driven out of his kingdom of Leinster by Roderic
O'Conor, king of Connaught, and chief monarch of
Ireland. Upon this he went over to Henry II., and
begged to have his aid in getting back his throne.
But Henry, although willing enough to aid one who
promised ever after to become a subject to himself,
was still too much occupied to come over to Ireland
at that time. However, he wrote a letter to his own
subjects, encouraging them by all means to assist the
exertions of the king of Leinster.

Chap. XXVII.—How the strangers came into Ireland; and how the Irish Prelates and Princes received Henry II. for their King and Lord.

AFTER obtaining this letter from King Henry, Dermod soon found persons in England willing to come over and fight for him in Ireland on reasonable terms, such as Richard Strongbow de Clare, Earl of Pembroc, Strigul, and Chepstow, Robert Fitzstephen, Maurice FitzGerald, &c.

Of these invaders, who were mostly Normans, the first party arrived at Bannow, in the county Wexford, under the leading of Robert Fitzstephen and others, in May, 1169. Others came soon after, and FitzGerald among the rest. At length, in May, 1170, Strongbow himself came, and was married shortly after his arrival, to Eva, daughter of King Dermod, a match which formed part of their agreement. These Normans were very successful in their expedition. Besides other exploits, they took Wexford, Waterford, and Dublin by storm, and soon restored in this way the sovereignty of King Dermod over Leinster.

About this time the clergy of Ireland held a meeting at Armagh, to consider what was bringing these calamities upon them, and giving strangers such power in the country. And they agreed that it was

a judgment upon them for their sins, and particularly
for buying and selling their fellow-creatures, the
English, for slaves. For the English people used to
sell their own sons and relatives in this way, and the
Irish were in the habit of buying them. And it was
therefore agreed at the meeting in Armagh, that all
such English persons should be allowed to go free.
One of the most famous of the Irish clergy at this
time was Laurence O'Toole, archbishop of Dublin, a
great friend to the Church of Rome, and the second
Irishman that was named a saint by her authority.

The arrival of Henry II. himself in Ireland took
place on the 17th of October, 1171. He landed at
Waterford, and spent fifteen days in that city. And
there, according to the arrangements which he had
made, there came to him the archbishops and bishops,
and other principal ecclesiastics of Ireland. And
they received him for king and lord over them, and
swore an oath of allegiance to him and to his heirs
for ever. And the princes of Ireland—as for instance
the Kings of Cork, Limerick, Ossory, Meath, &c.,
came also and followed the example of the clergy,
and received Henry for King and Lord of Ireland,
and became his men, and swore allegiance to him and
to his heirs against all men. The only Irish prince
of any consequence who opposed these proceedings
was Roderic O'Conor, King of Connaught; but he
also was obliged, in a very short time, to give up his
opposition, and submit to the King of England, as
the other princes had done. And in this way did

Henry the Second and his successors become, from
that day forward, the chief monarchs of Ireland,
which they have now been for 675 years, although
they did not become all at once possessed of that
complete authority over all parts of Ireland, which
they now enjoy. King Henry sent over the deeds of
submission of the Irish prelates to Pope Alexander
III., who succeeded to Adrian IV. And Alexander
gave his full sanction to these proceedings, and wrote
a bull confirming the kingdom of Ireland to Henry
and his heirs and successors for ever.

Chap. XXVIII.—About the Synod of Cashel.

ABOUT the same time King Henry, before leaving Ireland, gave orders that a council of the
Irish bishops and clergy should meet in the city of
Cashel, in order to make some arrangements for the
improvement of the church in Ireland. And accordingly the archbishops, bishops, deans, priors, and
other dignitaries of the church, assembled there,
early in the year 1172, and made such laws as appeared to them necessary. The person who presided
at this council was Christian, Bishop of Lismore, who
had been formerly Abbot of Mellifont, near Drogheda,
the first of the foreign-influenced monasteries that
had been established in Ireland by Malachy O'Morgair. Christian also succeeded to Malachy in the
office of pope's legate, which was the reason why he

was allowed to hold the chief place above the archbishops and other bishops in the Council of Cashel.

The laws made in this council were to this effect—
viz., that marriages should be regulated by the
church's laws; that infants should be properly and
publicly baptised in the churches; that the clergy
should have tithes duly paid to them out of the cattle,
corn, and other produce of their parishioners; and that
they should enjoy other important rights and privileges besides these; that wills were to be made according to a certain rule, in the presence of one's confessor
and neighbours, leaving half or a third of one's move-
able goods for the funeral obsequies; that these obsequies were to be accompanied by masses for the dead,
&c. And lastly, "that all church ordinances in all
parts of Ireland should, for the future, be regulated
according to the system of Holy Church, as observed in the Church of England."

These laws were confirmed by the king. They
were, as we may see, very favourable to the clergy,
securing to them tithes and other privileges of which
they had enjoyed little before, so as to make them
favourable to King Henry's government, and willing
to support his authority in their own country. Other
tithe-laws had been made before, but they were not,
as it seems, very much attended to.

There was also drawn up in the Council of Cashel
a letter on the state of the people of Ireland, com-
plaining that they were given to many enormities and
filthy practices, and had very little Christianity among

them. This letter was stamped with the seal of
Christian, the pope's legate, and afterwards trans-
mitted to Rome by King Henry, for the information
of his holiness as to the manners of our people.

Chap. XXIX.—*Pope Alexander's let-ters about Ireland.*

THE letter about Ireland and its inhabitants,
which was drawn up in the Synod of Cashel,
appears to be no longer in existence. But Pope
Alexander, immediately on receiving it, wrote back
in reply three very curious letters, which are still on
record. One was to the archbishops and bishops of
Ireland, one to Henry, King of England, and the
third to the temporal princes of this country.

In his communication to Christian and the other
bishops of Ireland, Pope Alexander tells them that he
had heard from their letter, and from other quarters
too, what an ignorant and immoral set of barbarians
the Irish were, having no fear of God, nor any regard
for the Christian religion : and that he was thankful
that God had put it into the heart of his dearly-be-
loved son in Christ, King Henry of England, to go
and invade them, and get them so famously under
his power. For that Henry was the man that would
stand up rightly in support of the church, as he had
showed already by his willingness to secure them the
tithes and other valuable privileges. For which reason he tells them to maintain the authority of the

King of England by all means, and excommunicate any person, princes or people, that would dare to raise any rebellion against him.

In the next letter, which was to King Henry himself, Pope Alexander tells him how delighted he was to hear of his magnificent victory over the wicked people of Ireland—people that had quite given up the fear of the Almighty, and were slaughtering one another to no end, and living in adultery with their near relations—people that made it a general rule to eat meat in Lent, and would pay no tithes, nor show any due respect for churches or clergy. "I believe in my heart," says he, "that it was to get pardon for your sins that made you undertake the trouble of having anything to say to such a people. Stir yourself, then," says he, "in this good cause, and do your endeavour to have them rightly instructed in the true Christian religion ; for that will promote their salvation and your own at the same time." Dr. Lanigan remarks, however, that Pope Alexander "seems to have known nothing of the state of the Irish Church, except what he had heard from the lying accounts of the enemies of Ireland." And certainly he could not have known much of it ; for at the end of his letter to Henry he speaks to this effect—" Your majesty is aware that the Church of Rome has a special right over islands ; and we feel quite sure that you would be desirous not only to support her authority where she has it, but also *to establish her power where she has none :* so that we would strongly urge you to be careful to secure us, in that land in question, the rights belonging to St. Peter, and *even if they are not allowed there*, that your majesty should see to enforce them, which will gain you our heartfelt gratitude, and be only a proper acknowledgment to the Almighty for your glorious victory."

In the third letter, to the princes of Ireland, the Pope tells them that he was very glad indeed to hear that they had received Henry for their lord and king, which he hoped would be much for the good of the country ; and he exhorted them by all means to be loyal and faithful to their new monarch.

Chap. XXX.—*Of the Church Policy of the . Anglo-Norman Settlers in Ireland.*

AND now that the Normans from England had gotten their power established and acknowledged in Ireland, they began, without loss of time, to turn the matter to their own advantage as fast as possible ; for they were very anxious to secure for themselves lands, and castles, and church-livings, and property of all kinds, in Ireland, whoever might be the owner, or however he might come by his loss. They began, we may see, by flattering the bishops and clergy, and securing their privileges, finding how useful a help they could be to them towards keeping the country quiet and in order under their authority. But there were still at this time several of the Irish bishops, and, perhaps, more of the clergy, who did not care much to obey the Pope, or uphold the new doctrine of his supremacy in Ireland, or the laws passed at Cashel by the sanction of his authority. In many parts of Ireland, as Dr. Lanigan observes, the Cashel decrees " were disregarded by the Irish clergy and people, who looked only to their own ecclesiastical rules, as if the synod of Cashel had never been held." And these persons had no liking for the English either, or their Church, so that in a short time there arose much disagreement and quarrelling between the two sorts of Irish clergy ; some loving the old Irish system, and the notions received from their forefathers, and some preferring the new system that was beginning to prevail. But the new system, under the support and countenance of the Pope and the English, was by far the strongest.

In order to strengthen their power in Ireland, the Norman invaders, who had seized on lands and plundered the Irish, began to build a great number of grand and splendid monasteries and religious houses in all parts of the country which came under their power, in order to educate persons in them under their own influence, to become bishops, abbots, and parish priests, in Ireland. And into these new monasteries they were, day after day, and year after year, bringing over numbers of monks from England, to educate the young people of the settlers ; for they would not trust them to the Irish to educate, nor did they want the Irish to be educated in

them at all. The old Irish monasteries were many
of them destroyed by the Danes, and others in a state
of decay. But the Norman strangers did not want
to help or improve these, or encourage them in any
way. They prepared for the national education of
Ireland a system that would be less Irish, and more
English and Romish, and one that would throw the
power and influence of the country more under the
control of the foreign governors. Some of the most
ancient and famous of these foreign-influenced monasteries were at Mellifont, near Drogheda; Bective,
in Meath; Boyle, in Roscommon; Baltinglass, in
Wicklow; All Hallows, in Dublin; Kilmainham
Priory, and the Abbey of St. Thomas, also in Dublin; Inch, Greyabbey, and others, in Down; Dun-
brody and Tintern in Wexford, Grace Dieu, near
Swords, in Dublin; and others without number.

The power and influence of the Norman settlers in
the Irish Church soon became very great, and they
managed ere long to get the chief bishoprics, the
richest abbeys, and the best church-livings into their
own hands, making rules to exclude the Irish from
them, and keep all the benefits of such offices to
themselves and their supporters and friends. The
Irish bishops and clergy who disliked Norman and
Roman influence, would also, at times, endeavour to
keep out the foreigners from such churches as were
under their influence; but here the Pope would interfere, and put a regular stop to such attempts at re-
sistance to the power of England.

Chap. XXXI.—Of Edward Bruce's War against England.

AND so, for about four hundred years after the kings of England had gotten power in Ireland, they and the popes agreed well together; and if they didn't manage between them to keep down well such of the poor Irish as attempted to struggle after their old independence, it's no matter. Those bishops and clergy of the Irish race who received most cordially the doctrine of the Pope's supremacy, and thought most of the Church of Rome, were, of course, their best helpers in this matter; and to them were added the new bishops, abbots, and other dignitaries, that were day after day appointed out of the new monasteries under English influence.

In the year 1315, about 150 years after the coming of the English into Ireland, the people of Ulster, wearied with seeing the oppressions and encroachment of the Norman barons who had settled in Ireland, became involved in a war against England; at least such of them as cared or dared to struggle any more for freedom; and to help their cause, and head their arms, they invited Robert Bruce to come over from Scotland, and become their champion. Robert, however, being unable to come himself, sent over his brother Edward instead—a bold and hardy adventurer, who gained some advantages, but was of little

use in the end to the cause of the Irish people; for
after having made the country desolate, and ravaged
it to a miserable extent, and after having been pro-
claimed King of Ireland, at Dundalk, he was at
length killed in battle there, in A.D. 1318. His war
ended in a most frightful famine.

The clergy who favoured the cause of the insur-
gents, and many of the Franciscan friars in particular, did all in their power, by preaching and
exhortation, to get the people to join Bruce in his
expedition. But those who were more entirely
under the influence of the foreign powers, England
and Rome, acted quite in the contrary way, and
made use of every exertion to put down the insurrection. For instance, the Archbishops of Cashel and
Dublin were appointed, one after another, to be at the
head of the Irish government during this war; and
when the battle of Dundalk took place, the Archbishop of Armagh, who was hated by the people on
account of his attachment to the Anglo-Norman
cause, was there with the English army, exhorting
the soldiers to be valiant against their enemies, the
Irish and Scotch, and giving blessings and absolu-
tions to all who should fall in the battle against
them.

Chap. XXXII.—*How the Irish complained of the English to the Pope, and what the Pope did thereupon.*

AND what part did the Pope take in this unfortunate war? This remains to be told, and is worth knowing. But first we must observe, that when the poor Irish, who had engaged in the war, saw how they were circumstanced, they thought it best to send a petition to the Pope, to endeavour to get some relief by his means. The doctrine of the Pope's supremacy had now been taught among them for nearly one hundred and fifty years, so that we need not wonder that they now received it as part and parcel of Christianity, as they were not taught to read the Scriptures, or otherwise instructed to the contrary. And therefore, although the introduction of the Pope's power into their country had been the means of bringing on them great harm and oppression, still, as they knew of no religious objections against the doctrine of his supremacy, or that it was contrary to the word of God, they addressed him as their chief spiritual pastor, in very humble and respectful terms. Their letter to the Pope was directed to him by "Donald O'Neyl, King of Ulster, and by right King of all Ireland, and the princes, nobles, and people of the same country."

In this letter, which was very long, they told the

Pope that their country had been thriving and
flourishing, gloriously and well, for thousands of
years, "until his predecessor, Pope Adrian, gave in
to the wicked suggestions of King Henry of England," and deprived them of their native independence, which they had enjoyed for ages, under a
long and unbroken line of their own kings, to give
them up, as they said, "to those crafty foxes and
ravenous wolves" from England, who were driving
them out of every good part of their own country,
and forcing them to take refuge in its wild moun-
tains and barren fens. "Since that time," say they,
"when the grant was made, more than 50,000 have
been slaughtered in war by the sword, and otherwise, in consequence of it. Such are a few circumstances, illustrating our former happy state, and the
miserable condition to which the Pope of Rome has
reduced us."

Moreover, the complainants informed the Pope
that the English were mad enough to require all
Ireland for their own property, and said that no
Irishman had a right to the freehold of any part of
it. And that the English monks and clergy used to
preach to the people that it was no sin to kill an
Irishman; and that if an English priest killed an
Irishman, he would say mass after, just as if nothing
had happened; and that any one else, who would
murder the best and most noble of the Irish, would
only be honoured and rewarded for it by the English,
and that not by the people only, but also by the

monks and bishops. And that all this was the reason why they were now determined to be free, and why they chose Edward Bruce for their king, an act which they humbly hoped that his holiness, Pope John, would approve of and sanction.

But the Pope was too much in league with England, and anxious to be on friendly terms with the English kings, to do much for their enemies in Ireland; so he gave orders to some of the bishops in Ireland to excommunicate by bell, book, and candle, Robert and Edward Bruce, and all their followers, and other enemies of the king, Edward II. of England. At the same time, however, he wrote a civil letter to King Edward, advising him, in common justice, to try and get some redress for the complainants. And he sent also to the king a copy of the letter from Ireland, and likewise of Adrian's bull, which the Irish had sent him, to call to his mind how little attention the kings of England were paying to the contents of it, about improving the morals of the people of Ireland, &c.

Chap. XXXIII.—How England and Rome agreed in putting down the Irish Language, Irish Customs, &c.

A GREAT many, however, of the strangers who had settled in Ireland, began gradually to like their Irish neighbours, and to adopt their customs and manners, laws and language, forming

intermarriages also, and other connexions with the
natives and their children. Such persons were
known by the name of degenerate English. But
their mode of life was very displeasing to some of
their countrymen, who were higher in influence and
authority, for they were afraid that this mixture
with the native Irish would greatly lessen the influence and respectability of the English settlers in
this country.

And therefore very severe laws were made, from
time to time, against the language, national manners
and customs, and general peculiarities of the Irish.
Of these legal enactments we cannot speak particularly here, except in one instance, which may be
noticed as an illustration of the kind of laws which
we are speaking of.

The *Statute of Kilkenny* was a very famous act,
or collection of acts rather, passed at a parliament
held in Kilkenny in the year 1367. By this statute,
marriage with the Irish, or connexion with them by
nurturing of children, or gossipred, or submission to
the Irish law, was to be considered and punished as
high treason. Also persons of English race were
forbidden to use the Irish language, Irish names,
Irish dress, Irish way of riding on horseback, &c. ;
and any English persons, or Irish living among
them, who should use the Irish language, were to be
punished with the loss of goods and imprisonment.
Also, none of the regular or mere Irish people were
to be allowed to any office of honour or emolument

in any cathedral, collegiate church, or religious house, where the English influence prevailed.

At the parliament that passed these laws against the Irish language, &c., there were present the Archbishops of Dublin, Cashel, and Tuam, and the Bishops of Lismore and Waterford, of Killaloe, Ossory, Leighlin, and "Clon," eight prelates in all, seven of whom had been appointed by the Pope, in consequence of the new powers acquired by him since his supremacy came to be acknowledged in Ireland. And these prelates all agreed in denouncing excommunication against any that would disobey this act ; nor did any of the other bishops of the island raise any voice of remonstrance against these proceedings.

The same system of discouraging the Irish language, and all Irish national peculiarities, with a view to bringing in English in their places, was followed always after in Ireland, while the Church of Rome had power here. The first encouragement to learn and teach the Irish language, and instruct the people in religion by means of it, was given in the reign of Queen Elizabeth, as we shall see more fully by-and-by. In the time of the good young Prince, Edward VI., before Elizabeth's reign, some little appearance of encouragement had been given to it already, but that was not, it seems, accompanied with any success.

Chap. XXXIV.—*Of the aspect of Religion in Ireland, from the Invasion to the Reformation.*

AS to the general state of Ireland and its people, from the time of the Synod of Cashel to the period of the British Reformation, the records of our history supply us with abundant proofs on that head, a very small portion of which, however, will be sufficient for our present purpose.

It may be said briefly, but very truly, that in those days Ireland was overrun with an amazing extent of ignorance, false doctrine, superstition, fighting, and every kind of disorder, among the clergy and laity in general. The Word of God was hardly known, read, or preached among the people at all in these times. The doctrine of the Pope's supremacy was generally received, in one degree or another, among all classes—by some cordially—by some carelessly. And it was the means of leading the people to embrace every dangerous and antiscriptural error which was taught or patronized in the Italian Church at this time. The merits of men's works, in building monasteries and abbeys, and endowing them with lands, were more trusted in than the sacrifice of the Son of God on the Cross, or the changing of the heart by the sanctifying of the Holy Ghost, of which the Scripture saith, "without holiness no man shall

see the Lord." Relics, and many of them pretended
and false, yet supposed to have belonged to the Lord
or the saints, were greatly sought after, and held in
honour beyond all measure. Images were adored
with wonderful veneration, and supposed at times to
speak, and work various miracles. The honor of the
Lord, who is a jealous God, was divided and shared
among the saints ; and while one cathedral in Dublin
was dedicated in the name of the Father, Son, and
Holy Ghost, the other was consecrated " to God, our
Blessed Lady Mary, and St. Patrick." Private masses
for the dead came into much reputation. Pilgrim-
ages and penances furnished matter for other super-
stitious abuses. The monks had become corrupt and
greatly degenerate. The begging friars, a new set of
beings, were propagating their modern system of religion, unheard of for 1000 years after the Apostles,
and by their impudent effrontery were persecuting
the better sort of clergy and laity, under the protection of the Pope of Rome. The bishops and archbishops, deans and abbots, priors, and other dignitaries, were guilty of profligacy and immorality, assaults
and violence upon one another, accompanied with
bloodshed, and even murder. Heretics and witches
were burned in the flames, and all who opposed the
tyrannical friars were threatened with the same treatment from the Inquisition. Excommunication was
used in revenge for personal quarrels, and indulgences
granted by prelates to those who would attack and
injure their enemies. And that the head and princi-

pal author of all these abuses might not be wanting
in decent means for carrying on his own wars abroad,
and other private purposes, vast sums of money were
year after year extorted from the clergy and people of
Ireland to supply the demands of the treasury in
Rome.

Chap. XXXV.—In which are plainly noted some of the first beginnings of Romish power in Ireland.

BUT the power and supremacy of the Pope in
the Church of Ireland was at length to come
to an end, as we shall see presently. First, however,
it will be no harm to go back a little, and endeavour
so to keep in mind the beginning of it also, that we
may have a better general notion of the matter, from
beginning to end, in one view.

First of all, for seven hundred years after the arrival of St. Patrick, there was no such thing as the
Pope's power in Ireland. Take all the Roman writers
that have ever written a book on Ireland, or the
Church in Ireland, and see whether any of them attempts to show a case of any one bishop appointed,
nominated, selected, or chosen by the popes to any
one see in Ireland in all that time; or any other
business of any kind whatsoever, in Ireland, meddled
or interfered with by them during all that period.
It cannot be done.

The first Irish bishops that ever were subject, in

any way, to any foreign bishop, were the Danish bishops of three cities of Ireland, already mentioned, in the year 1074, and afterwards. The first Pope that claimed supremacy or power over Ireland was Gregory VII., in 1084. The first pope's legate for Ireland was Gille, Bishop of Limerick about A.D. 1106. The same Gille was the first to endeavour to banish the old Irish Church-service books, and bring in the Roman mass in place of them. The first Irish Council at which a pope's legate presided, was that of Rathbreasail, in 1118. The first Irish bishop, whose appointment was at all influenced by a Pope of Rome, seems to have been a bishop of Cork, about A.D. 1140. The first Irishmen that got the name of saints, by the appointment of the Church of Rome, were, Malachy, who died in 1148, and Laurence O'Toole, who died in 1180. The first palls from Rome that ever were worn in Ireland, were those given to the four Irish archbishops by Cardinal Paparo, in 1152. The first council in Ireland which ordered the practices of the Church here to be regulated in accordance with the system of Rome, as used in England, was the synod of Cashel, in 1172 ; and the first primate of Armagh appointed by a pope was Eugene Mac Gillivider, in the year 1206.

Such were the steps by which the Pope's power came into this country, until at length he was able to secure the chief point, in raising taxes out of the land. For which purpose it was not long till he had a careful and exact list made out of all the parishes in the island, with the value of each, and the sums they should pay respectively to his treasury.

Chap. XXXVI.—About Henry VIII., Edward VI., and Queen Mary.

THE person that was the means of breaking up the Pope's power in Ireland was Henry VIII., king of England. At least he was the one to begin that work, although he was not the one to introduce, or even to embrace for himself, the Reformed Religion. For the establishment of *it* was a proceeding of a later time, begun by King Edward VI., and completed by Queen Elizabeth.

Henry VIII. was a bad man, governed by wicked and brutal passions, a cruel tyrant, and persecutor of many good men. But when the Pope treated himself unjustly, and tyrannized over him for a long time, he resolved to bear it no longer, but to put an end to the Pope's supremacy and taxes in his own dominions ; and this he did in England and Ireland by the help of the bishops, clergy, and influential laity of the two kingdoms. In Ireland, three archbishops, and many bishops, if not all in the island, swore against the Pope's supremacy. And all the native princes did the same, and supported Henry rightly in his opposition to the bishop of Rome—so that Ireland came into great peace and quietness in that reign. For the Irish princes liked Henry's government as much as they could that of any English monarch, and they did not care much about the power of the Pope. All other articles of the creed of Rome were, however, still held and agreed to by them, as well as by Henry himself.

Pope Paul was of course very angry at losing all his taxes and power in these countries, and he showed his fury by writing a long and terrible thundering bull against him, in 1535, declaring him infamous, dissolving all leagues between him and other Catholic princes, absolving his subjects from their oath of allegiance, encouraging them and others to make war upon him, cutting him off from Christian burial, and, in fine, consigning him to everlasting damnation. None of the Irish, however, seem to have minded all this very much, and Henry thrived and prospered under it extremely well. Although Henry VIII. himself cared little about real reformation or true religion, some others under him were more active in such works, during his reign. George Browne in particular, whom he had gotten appointed archbishop of Dublin, was very diligent both in his reign and that of his successor, in banishing ignorance and superstition, and promoting the knowledge of Christian truth.

On the death of Henry VIII., in 1547, his son, Edward VI., came to the throne—a good and pious prince, who showed every desire to promote true religion among his subjects. But his short reign ended with his life, in 1553.

Next came his sister, Queen Mary, whose heart was full of devotion to the Church of Rome, and her religion such as she had learned from it. In England she showed her feelings by promoting the torture and burning of the Reformers for heresy, as she and her party called their faith; and she would, probably, have done the same in Ireland had she reigned longer, as she had laws made for the purpose. But as she died after a short reign, her principal transactions with regard to this country were, the depriving of the reformed bishops of their places for marriage (*i.e.,* such bishops as had been appointed lately, of reformed principles, five or six in number, including Archbishop Browne), and restoring once more the Pope's power and the whole religion of Rome in this country, as it had been when her father began his reign.

Chap. XXXVII.—How the Reformation was established under Queen Elizabeth.

AND so it came to pass, that when Queen Elizabeth came to the throne in 1558, all Ireland was under the Church of Rome; the Pope's supremacy, and other doctrines of that Church, enforced in all places; bishops of her creed in every see; and religious affairs, generally, pretty much as they had been before Henry VIII. began to make any of his changes in the country.

One of the changes ordered to be made in Ireland in the reign of Edward VI., was the removal of the

Roman mass from the churches, and the introducing of the English service instead, with permission to use Irish where it was needed. But Queen Mary had repealed this ordinance with others, and brought back the Latin mass in all places. Now, the restoring of the English service was, on the other hand, one of the first steps to reformation adopted in Queen Elizabeth's reign. Those who loved Rome were much annoyed at this, and did all in their power to hinder the very first commencement of it; but their efforts were in vain.

The next thing of importance was to restore the laws that had been made against the supremacy of the Pope, so that the queen should have the same authority over all persons, lay and clerical, as the old chief monarchs, or other secular princes of Ireland, had always possessed in ancient times; and that she should be acknowledged head of the Church here, as they had been: not to preach, or administer sacraments, or interfere with the holy authority committed by Christ to the ministers of his Church; but to rule and govern the persons and properties of all kinds of people, clergy and laity, within her dominions; and that no foreigner should have liberty to interfere with them, to the damage of the power given to her majesty from God.

Accordingly there was a parliament held in Dublin, in the year 1560, at which two very important acts were passed: 1. One abolishing the usurped supremacy of the popes, and restoring to the kings of

England their ancient privileges, and those that had belonged to the old Irish monarchs. 2. And another called the Act of Uniformity, which ordered that the Book of Common Prayer, in English, should be used in the parish churches, and that all persons not having reasonable excuse should attend them on Sundays and holidays. By reason of these two enactments the reformed religion became the établished religion in Ireland, which it has ever since continued to be, although not always with the same support and countenance from the ruling powers of the state.

Chap. XXXVIII.—*How the Catholic Bishops of Ireland forsook the Pope, and embraced the Reformation.*

A.D. 1560.

AT this parliament there were present a large number of the Irish prelates, including all the archbishops of the day, and sixteen or seventeen other bishops—seventeen according to the best authority; and these archbishops and bishops agreed to the establishment of the Reformation, and gave their confirmation to the acts aforesaid; two prelates only excepted.

These two prelates were William Walsh, Bishop of Meath, and Thomas Leverous, Bishop of Kildare. They had both been irregularly intruded into their sees, by the authority of Queen Mary, while the former lawful prelates were still alive, after those prelates had been unjustly deprived of their places for being married men : and they were now both of themselves removed in like manner, for their determination to uphold the usurped power of the Pope, and excite opposition to the reformed religion. Leverous afterwards kept a school in Limerick ; but Walsh, who was more violent, was first imprisoned, and then banished.   He died in Spain some years after.

But the other bishops kept their places, and remained in possession of their sees, appointing, or consecrating rather, new bishops of the reformed faith, according as vacancies occurred ; and it is from them that are descended, by regular succession, the bishops of the present reformed, or, as some call it, the established Church of Ireland.   And no other prelates but those same reformed Protestant bishops, have any descent, by succession, from St. Patrick, and the bishops ordained by him and his fellows and followers in this island.

The Pope seeing his power failing in this way, was greatly exasperated against Queen Elizabeth, whom he looked on as the chief cause of these evils ; and, therefore, he did all he could to damage her, and excite her enemies to rebellion against her.   He excommunicated her, declared her a heretic, pretended to give her dominions to the King of Spain, and wrote bulls upon bulls to encourage her subjects to war upon her, telling them that it was as meritorious to fight her armies as to fight against the Turks ; and

granting the same indulgences, and full remission
of all their sins, to those engaged in the one cause
and in the other. And also in one of these insur-
rections against her, undertaken by the family of the
Geraldines of Munster, under his protection, he gave
pardon to a large band of Italian robbers, who lived
by plundering and waylaying the country people in
that land, on condition that they would come and
fight for the faith in Ireland; as we are informed by
the famous Romish historian, Philip O'Sullevan.

Chap. XXXIX.—*Concerning the Titular Bishops of Ireland.*

BESIDES the lawful bishops of Ireland, who had
been under the Pope's authority, and afterwards
gave up their adherence to him, and joined the Reformation, there were certain others also, from time
to time, appointed by foreign authority, of whom it
is right to take some notice in this place. These
were the titular bishops of Ireland, or bishops appointed, by the Pope's authority, to the name and
title of certain sees; not, however, consecrated by
bishops of the Irish Church, but by foreigners abroad,
and not allowed, in general, to hold the sees which
they claimed as their own.

At first they were only occasional, that is to say,
odd ones appointed here and there to particular sees,
where the Pope might not like the lawfully-appointed
prelates. There were some such appointed in the

G

reigns of Henry VIII. and Edward VI., and before
their days, but still more in Queen Elizabeth's reign.
They were, however, more of political and military
agents than clergymen. Many of them lived in foreign parts, or travelled from one country to another
for the business of war, and some of them fell in
battle at home.

One of the earliest and most famous of the titular
prelates of the times we are now considering, was
Robert Waucop, a Scotchman, appointed in the
reign of Henry VIII. by the Pope, to be Archbishop
of Armagh. Waucop sat as Primate of Ireland in
the Council of Trent, at the first session, and at ten
others; but though appointed by the Pope, and
received by what was called a general council, we do
not find that any of the Irish bishops, or clergy of
any sort, allowed him for their primate. On the
contrary, it seems they remained always faithful to
their lawful primate, George Dowdall, a respectable
and zealous prelate, and a great supporter of the
Church of Rome, although not, it would appear, a
favourite with the Pope.

On the death of Dowdall, the Pope appointed
another titular bishop for Armagh, named Richard
Creagh, in Queen Elizabeth's reign; and a kind of
succession of others after him in that see, and some
in a few odd ones of the other Irish bishoprics. But
none of these titular bishops were ever ordained by
the bishops of the Irish Church; they were consecrated by foreign prelates, the Pope in particular,

in countries beyond the seas, while the lawful succession was meantime regularly kept up in the Reformed Church of Ireland at home.

Some ignorant and mistaken persons have supposed (being misled by others who should know better), that Martin Luther, the German, had some power and authority in arranging the formation or reformation of the Church of Ireland; but it should be remembered that he was himself neither bishop, priest, nor deacon, of the Church of Ireland or England, nor a member of her communion at all, nor ever set foot in either country, whatever influence his opinions may have had in them. And it will be seen from what is aforesaid, that the introduction of the reformed religion into Ireland was the work of the lawful authorities, in church and state, of our own islands.

Chap. XL.—How Rome attempted to crush the Reformed Religion, by political troubles and war.

WHEN the reformed worship was first used under Queen Elizabeth, the people mostly had no great objection to it, and accordingly they attended, without much reluctance, the parish churches, where the English service was used. But the Jesuits, and other agents of Rome, who had lately come into the kingdom, used every exertion to draw the people away from them, calling the English liturgy heresy, and other worse names, and telling them it would be the destruction of their souls to attend there.

But these arguments, perhaps, would have had little influence over a large portion of the common Irish, had not political measures, rebellions, &c., been employed for the same object; for the people took too little interest in the temporal supremacy of Rome, and had too little objection to the English liturgy from religious motives, to be easily raised to insurrection about it. And, therefore, it was not till the queen was pronounced a heretic, and her subjects excited to war on her on that score, that the people attached to the Romish persuasion began to leave the parish churches, and continue separate, under the influence of Roman teachers, who managed, however, in the end, to form these persons into a new communion.

Hugh O'Neill, Earl of Tyrone, sometimes called Prince of Ulster, was the person appointed by the Church of Rome to be her military champion and head of her wars in Ireland, in the latter end of Queen Elizabeth's reign. He was one who had no more sense of religion than the horse he rode on, but being very daring, bold, and ambitious, he seemed very well suited to the work appointed him. The Pope and King of Spain favoured and helped him to the best of their power. He was, however, a bullying, tyrannical sort of chieftain, who forced the poor people, often much against their will, to

take up arms, and serve in his unholy wars. All
the hopes he could set before them, of getting rid of
the power of England shortly, were insufficient to
make them willing helpers in his work, or ready to
forsake their loyalty to the queen.

At length, after having involved all Ireland in war
and calamity for many years, he was at last brought
to complete submission, just at the period of Queen
Elizabeth's reign, was received in peace, and par-
doned. But afterwards he fled the country, and
retired beyond seas. His death occurred at Rome
in 1616. While he lived, the agents of Rome in
Ireland were continually encouraging the people to
hope that he would come back again, free the
country from the English, and establish in it once
more the power and religion of the Romish Church.
But the rumour that "Tyrone is coming," was
raised in vain, and at length came to nought.

Chap. XLI.—How there came to be Two Churches in Ireland.

ON the accession of King James I. to the throne
of England, matters were in a very unfortunate condition in Ireland; for, by the wars of the
Earl of Tyrone, which were then (in 1603) just ended,
the country had been overspread with desolation and
misery. Vast numbers had been slaughtered, and
the survivors made ignorant and brutish by the
habits of war. The churches were in a great many

places demolished and in ruins, and little appearance of religion left remaining.

The agents of Rome at the same time were busily working with the people, and flattering them to support the cause of Rome by arms. It is true the popes cared little about the common Irish, so long as they had the power of England on their side, and its monarchs of their faith ; but now the times were changed—the English would help the popes no more in crushing the Irish for their common purposes ; and so it seemed good policy to set the Irish against the English, by way of attaching them the more closely to Rome. This policy has been followed ever since, and with great success.

In the beginning of the reign of King James, the friends of Rome in Ireland used still to go more or less to the parish churches. And although there were one or two of those occasional titular bishops above-mentioned connected with the Romish party here, they had as yet no regular system of church government ; only they endeavoured to get the people to stay from going to church, and encouraged them to have mass said in various places, and be present on such occasions.

But at length, in the year 1614, when it was found that there was no hope of the government introducing the Pope's supremacy again, and no use in waiting for any change in the bishops of Ireland either, it was resolved by the Papal party in Ireland to have a complete establishment of their own archbishops, bishops, vicars-generals, deans, parish priests, &c., to be supported by contributions gathered among the people, as the church property was in the hands of the lawful prelates.

Accordingly, we find that, in a few years after this time—that is, in 1621—when Philip O'Sullevan published his "Catholic History" of Ireland, there were four titular archbishops for Ireland, appointed by the Pope, and ordained in foreign countries. In the other dioceses there were not bishops, but vicars-general, appointed to be over the clergy and laity of the Church of Rome in Ireland—that is, of that new branch of it which was thus formed, and has since continued in this island. Two of the archbishops lived in Ireland, and two in foreign parts : and the two who staid at home, and the vicars-general, assisted by the Jesuits and others of the religious orders, appointed new priests in the various parishes and dioceses throughout the four provinces of the country. Nor were they at a loss for young men to put into these places, as many had gone abroad to be educated in colleges in Spain, Flanders, &c., provided for the support of the Church of Rome by the exertions of her friends at home and abroad. Thus there came to be the two churches in Ireland,—the old one, descended from St. Patrick, now following the reformed faith, and this new branch of the Church of Rome, which originated in the manner here described.

Chap. XLII.—*Of the earlier Conventicles of Rome in Ireland, the Penal Laws, &c.*

BISHOPS and clergy of this new line of succession were now gradually provided, according as means and opportunities allowed, for all the dioceses and parishes in Ireland, until at length, after a very long time, they were all supplied with such rival pastors. And every means being used by the politicians and agitators of Rome to force the humbler classes, by persecution and exclusive dealing, to keep away from their parish churches and join these new congregations, the latter thus became very large and extensive, in the country parts especially. Although, in consequence of the strictness of the laws made against the power of Rome by the government in those days, these congregations were obliged to have mass celebrated in most cases privately, and out of the reach of the eye of authority, in private houses, or at mountain altars, or in secluded glens, exposed perhaps to rain, and wind, and weather. But the priests and friars who said mass in such places were very well paid by the people, and collected for their support immense quantities of cows, "garrons" or horses, small cattle, corn, &c. And in this way, and with money from foreign powers, the system thrived and prospered.

Still, at the same time, very severe laws were enacted against the power of Rome, and the proceedings of the clergy and religious orders, and many acts of cruelty and oppression were from time to time perpetrated, by persons who had power or opportunity, against priests and laymen of that persuasion. But we must observe a distinction between the laws, and the acts of private persons.

The principal laws made by Elizabeth and King James I. against Roman influence, were introduced for a just and lawful purpose—namely, to punish treason, and no⁺ to persecute religion. Priests were banished, or suffered other penalties, not for teaching transubstantiation, or the spiritual power of the Pope, or the worship of saints and angels, but for exciting the people to insurrection, and persuading them to join the King of Spain, who was at war with England, and fight for him against the government of their own country, and for helping to bring in foreign soldiers and officers, money and arms, from Italy and Spain, to maintain the pope's temporal power in this country ; as is very plainly confessed by the most learned and enlightened Roman Catholics themselves, by the famous and most learned father Peter Walsh, of the order of St. Francis, and others, bishops, clergy, and laity, of the Roman communion.

But as for any acts of cruelty that may have been perpetrated by private individuals, or particular magistrates, against members of the Church of Rome, peaceably inclined and loyal, such acts can only show that the doers of them were wanting in the spirit of Christ, not much influenced by His religion themselves, and ignorant of the right and proper way of promoting among their fellow-men the knowledge and love of evangelical truth.   Persecution can only make men hypocrites, never good Christians.

Chap. XLIII.—Of the Plantation of Ulster, &c.

IN pursuance of a commission issued by King James, in the summer of 1609, Hugh O'Neill, Earl of Tyrone, Roderick O'Donell, Earl of Tyrconnel, Sir Cahir O'Dogherty, Lord of Innishowen, and others, were convicted of treason and rebellion against the government, and their lands, extending through six counties of Ulster (Armagh, Tyrone, Coleraine, whose place Londonderry now occupies, Donegal, Fermanagh, and Cavan), and amounting to more than half-a-million of acres, were forfeited, and vested in the crown.

These lands being thinly populated, and in part quite desolate from war, King James made arrangements for bringing over large numbers of English and Scotch to occupy and colonise them ; hoping that, by introducing into the country such a number of persons of industrious and peaceable habits, and who would willingly take the oath against the supremacy of the Pope, the country would greatly improve, and his power there be greatly strengthened, by so many

loyal subjects being established in those parts. And
no doubt such a plan, whether just or not, might have
been attended with more good than has resulted from
it, if the parties who profited by these seizures had
cared more about religion or philanthropy, and less
about selfish ends and private gains.

Among the colonists were great numbers of Scotch
people, whose introduction gave occasion to the first
Presbyterian congregations in Ireland, in the year
1611. And in some parts the native Irish, who continued in attachment to the Church of Rome, never
seeing any other kind of Protestants, gave the name
of *Albanach*, or *Scotchman*, to all who professed a
reformed creed. But this name, although commonly
used in Ulster, at least by the ignorant, for all Protestants, is plainly an improper appellation for members of the Church of Ireland, and should be given to
Presbyterians only, no others being of "Scotch" religious principles or discipline. In other parts of
Ireland, the Irish term for Protestant is, in like manner, *Sassenach*—*i.e.*, Saxon, or Englishman. This
is used in places where the natives are mostly all Romans, and the only Protestants are descended from
English settlers. But the term is more correctly
used in this case, the persons so called agreeing to
the religious principles, and to the discipline of the
English Church, in accordance with the acts for the
Reformation of the Irish Church, passed with the
sanction of its own bishops, in 1560.

But to be a good, honest, and religious Protestant,

it is not at all necessary to borrow Scotch feelings or English feelings, or to forget any that are proper for a good and true Irish Catholic Christian. The true Irish Protestant will love Ireland, love what is truly national in Ireland, love the Irish people, their language, their welfare, their temporal and spiritual good, as considering them the children of a common country, the people of his bone and his flesh, and having a right to the warmest feelings and best affections of his heart. And if he refuses to acknowledge or submit to the usurped supremacy and erroneous creed of a foreign bishop, unwarranted in the Word of God, he does herein but follow the example set him by the best and holiest of Irishmen in other days.

Chap. XLIV.—Of the study of the Irish, the Holy Scriptures in Irish, &c.

GREAT many persons in past ages, and many of modern times, have, either from ignorance or malice, been led to regard with contempt the Irish language, and to discourage, either openly or secretly, the learning and study of it.

Some, who are ignorant of its value, regard it as a barbarous, useless, and mischievous tongue. They can stupidly delight in any fashionable nonsense connected with foreign antiquities, relating to Etruria, or Greece, or Kamtschatka; but wilful or invincible ig-

norance teaches them that the ancient annals and his-
toric records of our far more interesting and important country are not worth being made the subject of
inquiry.

And others of late days know the value of the
Irish language full well, but hating the light of history, which bears testimony against their errors,
would, as far as lies in their power, check and pre-
vent the study of this tongue, in order to support a
system rooted in ignorance and falsehood.

We have seen how, in the old Romish times of Ireland, this language was discouraged and suppressed
by the law of the land : a spirit of law-making which
prevailed until the time of King Henry VIII. But
in after days, from the reign of Queen Elizabeth especially, and subsequently, much has been done by
good men to encourage the communicating of instruction in this tongue to those who speak it, and the
study of it and of other matters of Irish History and
antiquity in general.

As regards the matter of the religious antiquities
of Ireland, no one laboured harder, or did more to
restore knowledge and information on the subject,
than the famous, learned, and pious Archbishop
Ussher, Primate of Ireland, in 1625. He was the
first to make a regular search into the old records
and lives of saints, &c., connected with this country ;
and the books which he published on this subject,
have been used and quoted since by men of all creeds,
who were indebted to him for information. Among

other treatises, he wrote a learned one on the *Religion of the Ancient Irish,* showing that it did not at all agree with that held and adopted by the Church of Rome. Members of the latter Church have also published some very learned works on Irish Ecclesiastical History, &c.; some of the most famous of whom are Father Colgan, Dr. Lanigan, the Four Masters, &c.

But none of our authors of those times are more deserving of being remembered with gratitude and love, than those who laboured in translating the Word of God into the mother tongue of our own island, for the Irish-speaking people. The two who first began this were two Dublin clergymen, named Kearney and Walsh, the latter of whom was afterwards made Bishop of Ossory. They were subsequently assisted by Nehemias Donellan, Archbishop of Tuam, who completed the Irish translation of the New Testament, which they had begun, and got it published in A.D. 1603.

And then came the venerable and holy Bishop Bedell, of Kilmore, in Cavan, who was the author of the translation of the Old Testament, in 1640. He was English by birth, but greatly loved and honoured by the Irish, bad and good, who hated England, yet could not but admire and reverence the piety and goodness of this excellent servant of God from that country. He was fifty-seven years old, when, for love to Christ and the souls of the Irish people, he first began the study of our own interesting, but most difficult, vernacular idiom.

If more of the Irish bishops and clergy, nobility, gentry, and people, calling themselves Protestants, had been such as Ussher and Bedell, the country would have been very differently circumstanced under their influence. The clergy would have been more faithful to their holy calling, and less lovers of the world; the landlords would have thought and spoken less about rents and game, upperwood and under-wood, &c., and more about the souls, and minds, and bodies of their tenantry; the people would have said less about Protestant ascendancy, and promoted more the ascendancy of holiness and true religion, of humility and love; and the smiles of gracious heaven might thus more willingly have beamed, with rays of blessing, on a prosperous and united people.

Any one who wishes to study the subject more at length, and to examine the references to authors, is referred to "A Primer of the Church History of Ireland," by the same author, lately published in Dublin.

𝕴𝖓𝖉𝖊𝖝,

WITH

REFERENCES TO THE CHAPTERS OF THE PRECEDING WORK,

Which may partly serve as an aid in finding out questions for examination in the Contents.

——————◆——————

H

THE END.

Dublin: Printed by EDWARD BULL, 6, Bachelor's-walk.

LaVergne, TN USA
09 November 2009
163550LV00004B/67/A